A Cast-Iron Aeroplane That Can Actually Fly:

Commentaries from 80 Contemporary American Poets on Their Prose Poetry

Edited by Peter Johnson

MadHat Press
Cheshire, Massachusetts

MadHat Press
PO Box 422, Cheshire, MA 01225

The Library of Congress has assigned
this edition a Control Number of
2019952008

ISBN 978-1-941196-92-2 (paperback)

Cover image:
Cover design by Marc Vincenz
Book design by MadHat Press

www.madhat-press.com

First Printing

For Russell Edson

Table of Contents

"A Cast-Iron Aeroplane That Can Actually Fly"[1]

When I was a young poet, one of my favorite anthologies was Alberta T. Turner's *Fifty Contemporary Poets: The Creative Process.* In 1977, when it was published, people began speaking seriously about the writing process, even in freshmen composition courses. What made Turner's anthology significant was that poets no longer feared that they might diminish their genius by describing how they wrote. Some of the poets in Turner's anthology even reproduced various drafts of their poems with original cross-outs and annotations, so we could see how ideas and strategies for poems came about. Their commentaries affirmed my suspicion that there was no one way to write a poem.

Turner's questionnaire was very specific, so much so that some poets refused to participate. They thought her questions were uninspiring or too rigid. One poet, whom she did not name, in a fit of hysteria, likened the questionnaire to something out of *1984,* which suggested how distasteful it was for some poets to discuss process. After all, one way to crown yourself a genius is to suggest that your poems are tiny gifts delivered by the gods in the wee hours of the morning, bestowed upon only special people, of whom you are one.

I was thinking about Turner's book when, in the last two volumes of *The Prose Poem: An International Journal,* I asked a few selected poets to choose one of their prose poems and to write a commentary on it. Unlike Turner, I didn't give much guidance. It would be nice, I said, to comment on it as a prose poem, but I didn't want to restrict anyone. As it turned out, many of the poets chose to discuss the prose poem as a genre anyway.

This anthology is an expansion of that project. I think it's a useful book. For one thing, it's a solid collection of prose poems written by some of the best American[2] practitioners of the genre. It also provides a good way of looking at the prose poem as a legitimate genre by focusing on what the poets themselves have to say. I agree with Michel Delville

1. The title of this anthology is from Russell Edson's essay on the prose poem called "Portrait of the Writer as a Fat Man."

2. The astute reader will realize that Michel Delville is a Belgian poet and literary critic, but because of his definitive book on the American prose poem and his own work in the genre, I have decided to bestow temporary dual citizenship upon him.

that one way to deal with the prose poem as a genre is to look at an "existing body of contemporary works labeled, marketed, or simply received as prose poems." Certainly what writers say about their work is important. If they call their poems prose poems and confess that they were self-consciously writing them as prose poems, thinking about a tradition that preceded them, then we should pay attention to that. If we find, as Charles Simic suggests, that he never thought of the short prose pieces in *The World Doesn't End* as being prose poems, then that, too, is significant.

Simply put, then, what follows is a conversation among many diverse poets on the composing of prose poems. I could fill ten more pages with a short history of how critics have discussed the prose poem over the years, but I would rather let these commentaries speak for themselves. If you are looking for a consensus of opinion on the prose poem, you are going to be disappointed. On a gut level, most of the poets included here would probably agree with Russell Edson that "What name one gives or doesn't give to his or her writing is far less important than the work itself." They may even agree with Friedrich Schlegel that "Every poem is a genre in itself." And yet, as the following commentaries suggest, hearing poets describe their writing processes can often situate their prose poems in a broader literary, historical, and cultural context, and may even help us to evaluate and appreciate their poems.

—Peter Johnson

Kim Addonizio

Watch

I wake up on someone's couch it's dark only a little moon through the window my skin cool and hot a man on me trying to push it in I'm too wasted I just let him he doesn't take very long. He gets off me and goes back through a door. I pull down my skirt go out to the street

walk blocks and blocks

a park huge dark trees men asleep on concrete benches

black woman in a leather miniskirt and silver boots asks me for a light. A car comes slow around the corner two men looking at us.

I start running finally I'm back at the apartment Jimmy's not there. I try to think if he was with me earlier. I've lost my keys. Ring Diane's buzzer she lets me in and gives me the extra set. In bed I try to sleep but the vomit comes up and I go to the bathroom and throw up then get under the cool shower water. I bring a pair of scissors back to bed. If I watch the door nothing will happen, no one will come. I curl up small and lie still trying not to breathe. I guess I fall asleep because Jimmy wakes me taking the scissors from my hand.

Commentary

"Watch" is from *Jimmy & Rita,* a novel-in-poems first published by BOA Editions in 1997 and reissued by Stephen F. Austin State University Press in 2012. Our current #metoo moment made me think of this particular poem, in which Rita, a sometime homeless woman addicted to alcohol and heroin, gets raped. When I wrote the introduction for the new volume, I noted the increasingly harsh economic times we were living in. Times seem harsher than ever for a lot of people, and homelessness and heroin are having their moment once more—not that it ever passed. I don't know if #metoo will ultimately have much effect on the power structures that ensnare us, just as I don't know whether literature about poverty or any of the other capitalist ills can transform the world. I guess the saving grace is that we can't know; our job as writers is to pay attention, and to speak, however and whenever we can.

Robert Alexander

Only in Retrospect

It's only in retrospect that you can say, "This was the last warm day of the year"—sometime in early October, before the storm clouds come sweeping in across Lake Superior and the temperature drops twenty degrees in an hour. But yesterday was one such day, a mild wind blowing from the south, a few leaves dropping from the multicolored trees.

More than a hundred crows flocked along the shore of Sable Lake, jawing back and forth into the morning air; two kingfishers flew upward into a cedar as I put my canoe into the water; out on the ruffled lake I saw a quintet of loons—flying south already?—and as I rounded the point near Towes Creek a bald eagle flew off from a maple and headed off down the lake. Though the crows were all about, they hardly seemed to notice: a few made cursory passes toward the eagle but almost, it seemed, pro forma, cawing in mild dismay—nothing, to be sure, like the way they mobbed an owl roosting outside my bedroom window one morning last winter.

In the afternoon I took my dog up to the Sucker River, and as we approached the high banks a single raven across the valley took off and circled overhead. By then the wind had died (only hours later it had shifted to the north and was building toward thirty knots), and we could hear the river gurgling like a broken faucet beneath us. Before us and around us and across the valley the trees stood motionless in their red and orange party clothes. Having worked all summer to store up food, and having been released till spring from the need to make a living, they were at last free to lose their green and stand for all to see in their true, most personal finery.

After another week or two and a few more north winds, the revelry would be over and they would strip down and go to bed naked, to sleep it off beneath the winter's snows.

COMMENTARY

What is poetry and if you know what poetry is what is prose.
—Gertrude Stein

For years I wrote prose poems without knowing what I was doing, thinking instead that I was writing some sort of shrunken, deformed story that I was too lazy to transform into a piece of *real* fiction. At that time, "prose poem" to me meant some sort of Dada-esque stream-of-consciousness vignette. This was long before the term *flash* had been applied to fiction in any but a marketing sense, and *short shorts* still referred to an item of clothing. One day, I decided to come out of the closet and to admit that I was, in fact, writing *prose poems.* This gave me the freedom to play with a mix of characteristics of tone and style and subject matter that were traditionally the realm of fiction writers, along with other elements that were traditionally poetic. That was the key to me: to be able to draw on the resources available to both novelists and poets.

The impulse of prose, it seems to me, is to tell a story—a story grounded in the real world—and this is true whether we are reading a newspaper, a letter, a biography, or a novel. This ability of the prose poem to take on various registers of language, its ability to masquerade as different sorts of literary or non-literary writing, is one of its distinguishing characteristics—what Margueritte Murphy calls (after Mikhail Bakhtin) its *heteroglossia.* But a poem is something else again. When we break a paragraph up into lines, creating free verse, the text immediately does more than simply tell a story. The context has shifted. The poem takes on airs, it has pretensions. Prose says: "Come listen. I alone have lived to tell this tale." But a poem entices us: "Come listen. No one else can tell this tale as artfully as I."

On the one hand, a traditional narrative is built up by slow degrees, layer by layer of impressions like an Old Masters oil painting; on the other hand, a lyric poem is like Zen calligraphy, all the creative energy stored like water behind a dam—or electricity in a Leiden jar—released in one burst of activity, lines on paper, the sense of the thing captured in just a few quick strokes. A plot means simply that something *happens* within a story, while in a poem all we can say for sure is that something is *happening*. The novel, or story, concerns itself with what physicists call the *arrow* of time—or the arc which any particular arrow follows—while the lyric poem focuses on what Buddhists might call the *suchness* of time, the way that things manifest in the moment.

In its essence the short prose piece, by whatever name, is a hybrid form, located at the crossroads of story and poem. On the one hand we can trace its lineage back through the whole universe of prose—fiction, nonfiction, memos and letters home—language that purports to tell us of the real world. Poetry, on the other hand—its history extending back through rhymed verse, blank verse, free verse—exists by its very nature beyond the realm of ordinary discourse; and this combination of opposites is what makes the prose poem so endlessly fascinating. While prose rises organically from the everyday, poetry with its long tradition of "nightingales and psalms" has about it something transcendent—and in this way the prose poem, child of two worlds, serves to bring together, for one brief moment, the sacred and mundane.

John Allman

Lunch

McDonald's: man in booth behind us obsessively at his wife, "Got to be black or white, black or white, black or white." In his sixties, in his anger; his wife nodding, her mind shut off, eye looking through the window behind him, traffic on Bedford Rd, the middle turn lane where Chevies wait. Children whooping two tables away: young mothers: half-copies of the *NY Times:* both toilets "Out of Order." *Beeping, beeping:* Home fries done. America engorging. America on the run. America: "Help Wanted." "That's what I said, that's exactly what I said. I did." Eileen and I: work to be done—front stoop, lighting fixture, white paint chalking down the brick wall: how many lawns to cut, trees to prune, rain gutters cleared of sludge, epoxy paint on old fridge, dog to walk, cats to feed, Eileen's father over each night in the second year of his loneliness. David arriving on the 15th with one of his children, Petra keeping the other just in case he won't return: wanting him to stay away forever, the children divvied up, her boyfriend's syringes tossed in the bathroom wastebasket, poor David tossed out, for what: keeping order. "I told you I would never do that again. I told you." That man, driving Eileen crazy. We move closer to the children. Shrieks. A boy racing up and down the aisle. We plan the day. We plan the next minute and the next. We plan never to stop planning. Swimming at Lake Canopus. Good wine. "I don't want summer ever to end."

Commentary

A prose poem possesses a vitality that defies boundaries, a kind of urgency in its flow, a freedom to span discourses and leap across vocabularies. It streams "subjects," showing how any moment is composed of simultaneities of place, time, consciousness. When I started work on "Lunch," I tried to keep the poetry camera on one event at a time, but the events were happening all at once. Only a prose poem could allow me to eliminate transitions or refocus.

"Lunch" is from *Algorithms,* a collection of prose poems published in 2012. If one thinks of an algorithm as the idea that, given a certain origin, a thing in process must become x or y, that tallies with the way most poems work, to achieve "form." But the prose poem seems to defy the notion of an ending. It simply stops, the streaming ends. Is there something missing here? After reading a prose poem, I find myself in a dreamy pause, not a conclusion. One algorithm implicitly leads to another. In short, I'm still in the flow, but wouldn't be there if an algorithmic process hadn't brought me into one.

Jack Anderson

The Marriage of Summer Hours

It was that bright warm summer Saturday in the square when everyone married everyone in the jubilation of brass choirs of auto horns and bouquets of sunlight drumming on golden walls, and a battered upright piano rolled into the very center of the space and a young man wearing a floppy hat with a feather in it sat down and played ragtime while an old woman hobbled by on a cane, grinning with delight and scattering breadcrumbs for the birds, and the little mossy fountain just couldn't stop giggling.

(Look, even now
after all that time

a few clear tears
of giddy summer laughter

stay moist on this page
and will not dry.)

*

Why shouldn't we be happy? Why can't we be?

Commentary

The most basic form of a prose poem is a rectangular block of words. But such units are ingeniously adaptable and arrangeable, and can become as complex and expressive as traditional line-and-stanza poems. It's also possible to combine elements of line-poetry and prose-poetry into hybrid forms, for instance, my "Marriage of the Summer Hours."

Today, line-poems are usually lyrics or narratives. But just as poets in the past wrote line-poems ranging from philosophical discourses to treatises on agriculture, so prose poetry permits the introduction of a host of supposedly "non-poetic" materials into poetry, thereby widening its scope. We can make prose poems out of orations, prayers, diary entries, lists, quizzes, instruction manuals—well, just about anything in fact or in fiction.

Although I have intentionally written a few poems that cannot be read aloud and I respect the tradition of the shaped poem that defies oral interpretation, poetry for me is primarily an oral art. Prose poetry can expand oral possibilities with its possible multitude of "non-poetic" voices. No author is compelled to use any of them, but there they are. In my own writing, I have never employed such venerable verse forms as *terza rima* or *dactylic hexameter,* yet I am pleased that they exist, ready for me should I want them; so, too, I am stimulated by the resources prose poetry makes available.

In addition to being a poet, I'm a dance writer and I've sensed likenesses between those arts, dance involving bodies moving on a stage, poetry involving words moving on the stage of a page. Printed poems may even be likened to one of our dance notation systems, all of which employ symbols to indicate bodily motion and dynamics. Unless one totally, and foolishly, ignores a work's appearance, its verse lines or prose paragraphs, sentence fragments, punctuation marks (or absence thereof), and word spacing can affect one's reactions in silent and in oral reading.

My hybrid "Marriage of the Summer Hours" was inspired by observing wedding parties in the town-hall square of Aix-en-Provence. The piece has three distinct units, each moving at its own pace, which I hope the distribution of words suggests. First, a prose-poem paragraph, a report of events, one after the other, in a single sentence. Although the reader cannot easily pause for a full stop, the narration does not rush; instead, I like to think that the words may amble.

After a break, a new unit, clearly line-poetry: three couplets in italics enclosed within parentheses, as if indicating that time has elapsed and this is a reflection on past events. These words could theoretically be arranged as prose, yet to different effect. I believe that the end of a poetic line, even if far from a grammatical stop, always prompts a shift of attention, possibly tiny, for eye or voice, before continuing. Try rearranging the lines in, say, W.C. Williams's "Red Wheelbarrow" or "Poem (As the cat)" and observe the different motional results that occur.

Finally, a break signaled by an asterisk, then one last line of—what? prose? poetry? No matter: it's obviously a conclusion. It looks like prose, yet it consists of two questions. So why join them, rather than keep them separate poetic lines? Because I wanted to show they were related and could dance together.

I didn't plan all this meticulously in advance. I just let feelings and ideas fumble around inside me, then shape themselves on the page. What came about was at least partially determined by the resources of prose poetry.

Nin Andrews

Spontaneous Breasts

All her life Rena had prayed to develop breasts. When she confided this to Barry Slick, the great Rishi, he informed her that she need only act as if she already had breasts. "It's all in your mind," he said. For seven days and seven nights Rena pondered. On the evening of the eighth night, a tremendous bosom flew out of her left side, soon to be followed by another on the right. A feeling of their presence filled the room, along with a soft white haze and the scent of rain. Rena could almost hear the breasts breathing. For many years after, Rena felt as if she were walking through a heavy fog with unexpected visitors.

Commentary

The idea for the poem and book, *Spontaneous Breasts,* first occurred to me when a friend, whom I shall call Rena, announced that she was planning to sprout breasts the natural way. At a meditation seminar she had heard of a healer who lived on the west side of Cleveland and who could hypnotize female clients, taking them back to their adolescence, thus stimulating dormant teenage hormones and inducing breasts to start growing again. After several months of visiting this healer, flat-chested women displayed major cleavage. The healer's name, if I recall correctly, was Dr. Slick. Rena confided to me how exotic her life with large breasts would be, complaining that she often felt as ordinary as a bowl of cornflakes. Privately, I imagined Dr. Slick as a tiny man in the midst of adulatory buxom women whose bosoms would never stop growing and whose hormones might never cease stirring. Although Rena was unable to locate Dr. Slick, she continued to relate his miraculous powers with breasts. And I started rewriting her life as if she were a victim of immense and instant breasts.

Because of poems like "Spontaneous Breasts," people often tell me I'm a surrealist, suggesting that my poetry is not of this world. My inspiration, however, often comes directly from experience, and I believe it is sometimes in the surreal that we recognize ourselves. Why? Because people are quite surreal, especially when it comes to their desires. Deep down many of us seem to believe that there is some kind of magic, a secret recipe, lover, prayer, or, in the case of Rena, a big bosom or two, that could deliver us whatever we wish for, that could transform us from Cinderellas into queens, from humans into angels, from couch potatoes into Olympians, from frigid souls into athletes in bed. Of course, advertisers feed on our unconfessed beliefs and yearnings, selling us potions, gowns, diets, drugs, faiths and mantras of every flavor, species, and dimension. There are, after all, so many seductive myths, parables and fairy tales of both positive and negative transformations, how can we resist them?

Perhaps Simone Weil was correct when she said that one of the first things we know about ourselves is our imperfection. Perhaps the second thing we know about ourselves is how much we yearn for perfection. But what is perfection and where does it exist? In a museum, a snowflake, California, or in a poem or another realm? How close can we get to perfection before falling like Adam and Eve from Eden? How many of the rough edges of life need to be smoothed away before perfection and beauty occur, and how do we know when we've erased too much? Would we be happy if we were perfect, and is it possible to segregate perfection and imperfection? Do we actually have an unconfessed love for our imperfection, or our untransformed nature? Will Rena be transported with joy by her big breasts?

These are the kinds of questions which inform both the form and content of my poems. My vision or concept of prose poetry is of a genre which does not claim to be either this or that, fiction or poetry, but which is both and neither, attempting an impossible balancing act between the polarities of our human nature and our aesthetic aspirations. Because we are both the people of our dreams and the strangers and neighbors others meet on sunlit sidewalks, I think it's only natural to seek a literary genre that is, at once, mystical and ordinary. Just as many poems might be better off maintaining the verbal magic and mystery of poetry while retaining simple prose structures, Rena, herself, would probably have been happier if she had only dreamt of, yet never achieved, her ideal form. Part of the beauty of prose poetry is its plainspoken elegance and the very question its existence poses to our concepts of the ideal, our models or standards and structures.

Sally Ashton

Gratitude

The woman woke from her nap. A breeze tossed through the greeny branches overhead. Some bird wheedled in a way that matched the motion of the wind, the leaves. A stem of grass teased her bare ankle. The dry air buzzed. In one direction a vineyard unfurled, rising, falling with the hills. In the other the steeple and tiled roofs of some small town stood almost asleep. She didn't want to move either. It was good that dinosaurs were extinct. They would have ruined everything.

Commentary

What if a time warp allowed dinosaurs to trample your idyllic summer afternoon? Or let you hang out with Einstein or Da Vinci? Or what if by squinting just a bit, you were able to see the uncanny, the absurd, or even the remarkable in an unremarkable moment? Or see yourself living someone else's life? Or vice versa?

Several of these "what-ifs" helped shape "Gratitude," a piece from my forthcoming book, *The Behaviour of Clocks,* a collection of prose poems trying to make sense of the space-time continuum. Yes, a daunting proposition. Einstein himself tried to simplify his concept of relativity through descriptions of clocks and trains. Playing with his models, I hope to capture fractured experiences of time, space, and motion to try and approximate aspects of his thinking. "Gratitude" is one prose poem in my kaleidoscopic attempt to "obtain a reasonable definition of time." Set in the suspended-time of lucid dreaming, the poem's tension arises in the friction between the fantastic and a woman's desire to simply be able to take a nap in peace for once.

The prose poem is well-suited to this playful venture, though I say that in hindsight since I began this piece and most of the collection *as* prose poems. While I don't blame a 10-year stint teaching freshman composition with its fixation on the grammatical sentence for my admiration of the prose poem's unbroken line, I do often find myself impatient with line-break and expect more than artifice. I want impact, i.e., "Where's the fucking *duende?*" With a prose poem I look for similar syntactical tension and release but by means of sentence craft, striving for a measured, shapely energy.

And I do find the prose poem's more plebeian, approachable form energizing. I love its invitational quality, like a note intercepted in class, or a postcard sent from abroad. Or a text message. What's inside? Its unassuming shape, disarming if not compelling, impels the prose poem's subversive power and surprise.

For me the form remains continuously agile and as American as Whitman's own untethering of the sentence in stand-alone lines. There remain new ways to play and expand, to morph with our cultural moment and its technologies, and to push the limits of genre. In its freshness framed in a familiar form, the prose poem—or flash fiction or nonfiction shorts for that matter—destabilizes fixed, often limiting notions of what poetry, and even genre, can be.

What if?

Michael Benedikt

The Doorway of Perception

If it was one thing he knew—even standing outside in the yard—it was that the universal problem had to be solved, the Doorway of Perception opened, behind which, despite the extraordinary demands he often made of himself, he still felt trapped in the vestibule of mimicry. So he knocked on the door. But no one opened it. He tried the knob, but it seemed to be stuck. (He thought he heard a tumbler start to click inside the lock—but then it stopped). He bent down and attempted to pick the lock using the keys from his own apartment door—but of course that produced absolutely no result whatsoever. Impatiently, he arose, walked back across the yard, and threw all his weight against the door from fifteen feet away! ... but for some reason, that didn't work either. Again and again he tried to break through that damned door, running at it across the yard from still greater and greater distances, but time after time nothing happened—except that the last time he threw his weight against it, the entire building came crashing down around it! And still, the door stood. Slowly, he backed up a dozen yards to the furthermost limits of the yard, which was surrounded by a fence; and once again he launched himself at the door—but this time only succeeded in smashing his spinal column! Finally, from his brand new wheelchair, he tried nuclear dynamite. The earth fell down around the door; he realized that the sky was falling—he actually moved both Heaven and Earth! Just before they fell, he managed to peer at eye-level from his wheelchair through the keyhole. But all he saw back there was someone holding up a small hand mirror—the tiny, inexpensive kind they sell at dime stores; and, in the center of the mirror, directly opposite the keyhole and looking directly back at him, was an eye.

Commentary

"The Doorway of Perception" is a poem about the necessity of occasionally getting outside the confines—liberated of course as they probably are—of one's own perceptions. After all, avoiding Solipsism—a universal problem, and obviously a particular challenge for artists in general if they want to communicate beyond a small circle of friends and admirers—is something that one's own critical faculties as a poet demand of oneself; and also something that even psychologists, who seem to be fundamentally indifferent to matters of esthetics, generally recommend as an essential—indeed a *sine qua non*—of good mental health. Since the temptation to be purely private when making utterances in such an off-the-beaten track medium as poetry is so great, trying to avoid Solipsism is, I think, particularly important for poets if we want to communicate clearly, without relying on an elaborate critical apparatus in order to get a point across. What I'm saying in the poem, in short, is that—self-exacting as many poets try to be—even with the very best will in the world, the task of avoiding Solipsism, and getting outside oneself, isn't very easy. (It's always kind of fun, though, isn't it!)

Incidentally, "The Doorway of Perception" is a poem from my fourth collection of poetry, *Night Cries* (1976), which—speaking of art on a (still, alas!) somewhat off-the-beaten path—is a book of prose poems. *Night Cries* begins with a quotation from Nietzsche: "Sawest ever thy friend asleep? Wert thou not dismayed by thy friend looking so? O, my friend, man is something that hath to be surpassed." Most of the poems in *Night Cries* are at pains to explore the ramifications of that simple, but—I for one think—truly immense idea. Quite a few years before, Harold Bloom wrote about this idea; the poem also, I guess, has something to say about "The Anxiety of Influence."

Robert Bly

A discussion of Robert Bly's "Warning to the Reader" from an interview with Peter Johnson in *The Prose Poem: An International Journal.*

Peter Johnson: Do you think that prose poetry more than verse poetry allows for the leaps we've been speaking about?

Robert Bly: I think a lot about the word "safety." One reason I couldn't write as well when I was twenty-five as I can now is that I didn't feel as safe then. At twenty-five you think you're going to do the wrong thing, and you probably are. You meet people who belong to the class system and are hierarchical, and this fear cuts down your ability to play. Instead of playing, you're looking for the right associations, the ones an educated person might have. I don't want to make a big thing about this, but for me one of the joys in the prose poem is that I don't feel as much fear there. I'm writing in a new form, so to speak; I'm not claiming that I'm keeping up to great standards. As I've said, the most wonderful thing about the prose poem is that no one has set up the standards yet the ability to make leaps has something to do with how safe you feel because if you can't feel safe, then you can't go back to your childhood.

PJ: There are some wonderful sounds in your prose poem "Warning to the Reader." That poem seems to me to be your *ars poetica.* The poem is a warning to readers and to writers, and it works so well because of its shifts in thought, especially the huge transition signaled by "But" in the second paragraph. I also think it's one of your darker and more ironic poems. What do you have to say about this prose poem?

Warning to the Reader

Sometimes farm granaries become especially beautiful when all the oats or wheat are gone, and the wind has swept the rough floor clean. Standing inside, we see around us, coming in through the cracks between shrunken wallboards, bands or strips of sunlight. So in a poem about imprisonment, one sees a little light.

But how many birds have died trapped in these granaries.

The bird, seeing the bands of light, flutters up the walls and falls back again and again. The way out is where the rats enter and leave; but the rat's hole is low to the floor. Writers, be careful then that by showing the sunlight on the walls not to promise the anxious and panicky blackbirds a way out.

I say to the reader, beware. Readers who love poems of light may sit hunched in the corner with nothing in their gizzards for four days, light failing, the eyes glazed.... They may end as a mound of feathers and a skull on the open boardwood floor....

RB: Well, the thought or drive of the poem is clear. I say I feel some responsibility through the years for urging readers to look upward, follow Kabir upward. I love ascents—who doesn't love ascents? But still, the old tradition was, no step upward without a step down. No food for the angel without some food for the rat. In *Silence in the Snowy Fields* I say:

The leaves at the crown of the tree are asleep
Like the dark bits of earth at its root.

But the main feeling in *Snowy Fields* is "the joy of sailing and the open sea!" The great joy is to follow the route of Kabir upward to that warm union he so marvelously evokes. Freud is a rat person. Freud is not popular now. It's painful to know how imprisoned our parents and grandparents were—how they couldn't see either the cracks in the walls, nor the rats' holes. With "a mound of feathers" I'm thinking of many unlucky friends in the ashrams.

If we turn and look at the sound now, I can remember writing and rewriting this poem, and deciding very early on the *n* sounds. "Sometimes farm granaries become especially beautiful when all the oats or wheat are gone." One can say "after the oats or wheat are gone," or "after the oats are hauled away." I had hundreds of possibilities, and settling on *n* helped narrow them down.

PJ: Don't you think those word choices are not really choices, that the right words often just arrive? Is it really such a conscious process?

RB: It wasn't so much a word, it was a sound. "… [A]nd the wind has swept the rough floor clean. Standing inside, we see around us, coming in through the cracks between shrunken wallboards, bands or strips of sunlight. So in a poem about imprisonment, one sees a little light." I remember having eight or nine possibilities for the adjective for "wallboards." Wallboards are boards that have been in the sun too long, and they actually become warped and smaller. So we understand there are always dozens of possibilities; but because of the *n*'s, I chose shrunken. The last sentence, "So in a poem about imprisonment, one sees a little light" came in during about the fifteenth rewrite.

PJ: I think that sentence is the core of the poem.

RB: Yes. I'm declaring that this poem is not really about nature or farm granaries. "How many birds have died trapped in granaries" that are workshops or meditation retreats that seem to offer life all the time, seem to offer constant glimpses of the spirit. "The bird, seeing the bands of light, flutters up the walls and falls back again and again."

PJ: And then we encounter another big shift.

RB: Yes. As I've said, there's a problem in all this fluttering toward the light, because the "way out" is really where the "rats leave and enter." Baudelaire was a rat. Remember his *Flowers of Evil.* "But the rat's hole is low to the floor." We're citizens of such a great country, why should we bend and go through a rat's hole? "Writers be careful then by showing the sunlight on the walls not to promise the anxious and panicky blackbirds a way out."

Then I decided to repeat the warning: "I say to the reader, beware. Readers who love poems of light may sit hunched," and I'm coming back to the *n*'s, "in the corner with nothing in their gizzards for four days, light failing, the eyes glazed.... They may end as a mound of feathers and a skull on the open boardwood floor...." Some academic poets too "sit hunched in the corner with nothing in their gizzards for four days, light failing, the eyes glazed." I'm not mocking academic poets; I'm saying it is difficult to have to teach ascensionist literature day after day. Ministers and priests suffer from it. So do I. So I had to finish the theme as best I could, but I also had to finish the poem musically with the *n*'s in the last sentence because that's where I began.

Greg Boyd

Edouard's Nose

Edouard doesn't have a head. A torso and limbs, but no head. Facial features in the middle of his back. He smokes a pipe, which he keeps in his mouth most of the time because it's awkward for him to reach his arms around to the middle of his back. "*Ceci n'est pas une pipe,*" painted Magritte, an allusion to the idea that the symbol does not necessarily correspond to the actual physical reality it's intended to represent. Same goes for the word nose and for the name Edouard, etc.

So much for background information. One day Edouard decided to take a walk. He put his nose on a leash and set out for the park. By the artificial lake he shared a bench with a woman with only one leg. "May I pet your nose?" she asked.

"Certainly," he replied, "but be careful, he's not always nice. Would you like a Kleenex?" he added, taking one out of the box he carried with him.

"No thanks, I'm on a diet," she said, so he ate it himself as she stroked his nose. "Nice nose," she said when it dripped on her hand.

She caught him staring at her missing leg, though there was nothing to stare at. "It's an old football injury," she explained, pointing at the nothing. "By the way, if you don't mind, if it's not too personal, what happened to your head?"

"Problem with my nose. Complications in surgery. Had to amputate." Edouard sighed and lit his pipe. "Dreadful business."

They talked like this for several minutes. By chance they met again in the same place the next day. In time they became lovers. She started wearing more revealing clothes and got her nose pierced. He took up tarot card reading as an exotic hobby. They rode nude together on a bicycle through the streets of Paris in the early morning.

They both claimed to have a total disregard for symbols. Neither of the two would admit to being in love. "Love my nose," said Edouard. Socially they were a big hit. It was fashionable to be seen at the same restaurant as Edouard and Edouardetta. Everyone ordered boiled nose. That was before the war, when nose was still plentiful.

Commentary

Like Edouard above, who expresses "a total disregard for symbols," the prose poem itself often noses its thumbs at linguistic convention. Since prose is based on the logic of an agreed-upon set of symbols, readers of prose trust that a particular word, "chair" for example, will not be used to convey the notion of "fast food" or "umbrella." Poetry undermines this expectation; for the very nose of poetry is metaphor, comparison via the substitution and subsequent fusing of unlike elements. Thus, in prose my love is a beautiful, accomplished, intelligent woman, whereas in poetry she may be a flower, a blowfish, a lawnmower, a nose.

The humor, paradox, irony and playfulness inherent in many of my favorite prose poems results from a head-on collision between the routine linguistic expectations of prose and the intensely lyrical disruptions of poetry. I take particular delight in how the very shape of the prose poem lulls and attracts the unsuspecting reader, who often wades into it expecting the calm waters of the familiar, only to find himself caught in a linguistic riptide.

An unleashed metaphor will wander, tail wagging, from place to place. In short, it will follow its nose. Many of my prose poems start with a metaphor and quickly expand it into its own universe. Each of these miniature worlds has its own unique physical laws and properties, its own logic.

Because they are generally short, highly concentrated narratives, prose poems make wonderful vehicles for a nosy imagination.

It occurs to me that the hero and heroine of my prose poem are both amputees. Edouard has "lost his head," while Edouardetta is missing a limb. Is this some kind of oblique commentary?

I smell a nose.

John Bradley

Mortal Colors

for Jana

Gray, white, brown scoured November sky. You were wearing a gray coat with round white circles, each one held by a tiny gold safety pin, trembling in the wind. The dog with the electronic collar silently racing to the end of the lawn, where the sensors lay buried out of sight. Halting to hurl his carnivorous cry. "*Anger, like sex, is quite sexual,*" the dog said, translating for us motion into language. Into private prophecy. Gray, white, brown, the bristles in my elementary mustache. "*Everything in the world exists to end in a book,*" my mustache said, translating color into urgency. Into shades of public privacy. You blew to me from the bare trees. Gray, white, brown strips woven by wasps into a wind-ravaged papyrus nest. "*Everything you say will be used by someone or something to fashion the walls of a home,*" the wasp colors said, translating specificity into curve. Curve into nonbinding text. The book that declares without declaring itself the first and last book. You will be wearing a nightgown with a round hole, a little bigger than a host, just below your navel. Do I place there my eye or my tongue? Either way, you and I will be read. Everything comes to this. Gray, white, brown, that's why I let them roam your humming hair.

Commentary

This prose poem started out as a verse poem so awful I have destroyed every version of it. It began, I think, like this:

> Gray, white, brown
> scoured November sky.

You can see the problem. I thought that only the colors were important. Those colors I saw that November day in Bloomington, Indiana: the gray, white, and brown of the wasp nest the same as those in my wife's hair. As a writer, I was operating on the belief that "condense, condense, condense," as Lorine Niedecker phrases the gospel of Ezra Pound, was the way to proceed. But, as I soon discovered, the haiku-like form (several stanzas of three lines) could not accommodate the experience. I returned to the poem many times, adding and then subtracting further detail, and coming away each time frustrated with the piece. Yet I was unable to dump it altogether.

A year or two later I decided to try a prose-poem version of the same experience. Suddenly the context entered the poem—the dog with the electronic collar that lived on the same road as the wasps. A dream of my wife with a hole in her nightgown brought out the sensuality of the colors in the wasp nest. And as the prose poem grew, I made a startling observation: My mustache had the same color as the wasp nest and my wife's hair! Now I was implicated in the "mortal colors." When this happened, I knew that the poem had finally arrived at its real destination.

Would this have happened if I had stayed with the tight, condensed form? I don't think so. It was only when I began working with the long line and open form of the prose poem that I felt permission to bring in seemingly non-essential material which enabled me to follow the arc of the poem. The prose poem's inclusiveness was ideal for this particular experience, though I never would have guessed that when I first began. One of the miracles of the prose poem is that it can accommodate *anything*, making it the most "modern" of literary forms, I believe. Certainly some "condensing" takes place as I edit my prose poems, but the (self-?) imposed restrictions of the verse poem, the need to strip away everything but the "essence," never allowed me to make the larger and more interesting connections that were inherent in the colors all along.

Joel Brouwer

Aesthetics

Your brother has leukemia? Carve ivory. The elections were rigged? Write a villanelle. A girl shivers in streetlight, takes off her mittens, pulls a silver yo-yo from her pocket. Dogs bark behind a fence. Use oil on wood. Concentrate on pacing when choreographing your divorce; you will have to move through it forever. Two men in green fatigues tie a woman flat to a metal table. One has a rubber hose, the other a pliers. A third man arrives with sandwiches and a Thermos. A body has soft and hard parts, like a piano. Music comes from where they meet.

Commentary

In the mid-1990s, I was writing the poems that would become my first book, and as is customary in such situations, feeling frequently that I was a failure and a hack. For distraction, to loosen up, to blow off steam, I started writing some prose poems, which I would turn to and take refuge in when I couldn't face the "real" poems that were giving me so much grief. In the end, probably unsurprisingly, the prose poems written for fun turned out to be stronger than most of the "real" poems. My second book collected the fifty best of them.

It may say something dire about my personality that my larky, telos-free diversion was premised on a comically severe restriction: These poems were exactly 100 words each. Yet "In truth the prison, into which we doom / Ourselves, no prison is," and indeed I found solace in the fixed square footage of my narrow rooms. I was born in late June under the sign of the crab. A friend claims this accident explains my fondness for submarine movies, cameras, peepholes in hotel room doors, camper vans, and rectangular prose poems. I like to be inside a snug space, looking out.

Everything pleasurable involves tension and release. Poems in verse use lineation to produce this dynamic. Denied line breaks, prose poets use syntax to (literally) take up the slack. I wrote prose poems on many subjects—war, love, art, fear—but their common fascination was good old-fashioned sentence variety. "Aesthetics" is a mean little screed about art's inability to counter so-called "real life." No villanelle ever stopped a coup. But ironically, or perversely, the poem's also about the very real pleasure generated by juxtaposing a hard imperative and a more discursive sentence's softness. Music comes, I hope, from where they meet.

Mairéad Byrne

The Russian Week

Inside this week is another week & inside that week is another week & inside that week is another week & inside that week is another week & inside that week is another week & inside that week is another week so that instead of 7 days each week is actually composed of 7 weeks each one a little smaller than its container week but still workable & with rosy cheeks. This arrangement is necessary. If a week were only a week *aka* a standard 7-day week it would not be possible to get things done. Therefore *voilà:* The Russian Week. As soon as it becomes apparent that everything cannot get done in the albeit larger, more commodious week, one can simply crack open the inside week, only slightly less commodious in size. Then, when things pile up as they are wont to do, one proceeds to the inside-inside week, its size only slightly less commodious again. And so it goes. I will not go through the process in tedious detail. For that it would be necessary to have an inside-inside-inside-inside-inside-inside-inside week, i.e., 8 weeks in all and obviously that is impossible. There may be some future in developing a system whereby each of the 7 weeks which constitute the week would in turn contain 7 weeks, giving 49 weeks in all inside one week, and indeed the prospect of an *ad infinitum* progression. But this proposal lacks the calm symmetry of the established model. It is knobby & hectic where the other is smooth, rounded, generous, economical—and natural. Thank God for the Russian Week.

Commentary

I've written hundreds of prose poems and have a dozen on hand ready for publication. So why pick this one, already published many times?

When I wrote it, in 2004 or 2005, I thought it a useful thing, a conceptualizer for the time challenged, almost as good as a machine. It doesn't quite work as a deliverer of internal resources but it almost does. It works as a poem for me. It has all the repetition in the world but still has a beginning middle and end. It involves numbers, which I like. It has its own logic, the sort of logic I appreciate. It's fun to read. It sounds a lot like poetry, also a puzzle and a spell.

Back then, when I wrote prose poems, all the edges, top, bottom, and sides had to be straight and sheer. I'm still obsessive about justification. I sometimes write poems in lines, or dialogues for two voices, and then reformat them as text blocks. My first gig as a writer was in magazine journalism, doing theatre reviews. There would be a press shot of the show and underneath, an equivalently-sized box for approximately 300 words. I thought I could make anything happen in that box. It was its own theatre.

I often write prose poems in sets, but "The Russian Week" is *sui generis.* It still evinces many of the features typical to my prose poems: time, numbers, neat solutions to tricky dilemmas, and self-reflexivity. I feel bad for not offering the opportunity of anthology publication to one of my more happening end-of-the-second-decade-of-the-twenty-first century poems. But for me this spanking lean and mean poem still has the edge.

Maxine Chernoff

Singular

Death's outlet song of life ...
—Whitman

Every man should be so much an artist that he could report in conversation what had befallen him.
—Emerson

High-mindedness is a construct of mind and its metals, its iron and zinc, its blue mercury.

It is a waste to consider how we relate to the human condition—we are the human condition in cotton and lace and charms that fit in thimbles. We are broken and fixed. We are mended and torn. We are the underlining of the soft belly of kangaroos crossed with examination books. We tell jokes that aren't funny and laugh with our eyes closed. When we open them, someone has died and another been born.

We praise Jove. We praise Allah. We praise the mark-downs at the Nordstrom Rack where a handsome young woman was weeping into her hands. We praise the immaterial essence of clouds that resemble your uncle on Wednesday. We praise the material grace of your hand on my collarbone, soft in its landing there.

We are unkind to our neighbors. We cheat on our friends. We are witnesses to the first bee in the jasmine we planted at noon. We are witnesses to the harms of a life and its slow repetitions that lead to new beauty. We travel to see peasants enact old rituals that we would find foolish in our own doorways. We are peasants as well under our skirts and children and finally fools. Who knows the height of a well-built arch or the dimensions for travel to Mars? They say if you fly there, you cannot return. There are those who will fly there. I heard them on a show discuss how they'll grieve for irises and children and the small fond expressions of those that they love.

We all leave cathedrals and ashes and bony candles burnt to their wicks. We all leave nothing we wanted and everything we did and that of an in-between state of a small conversation involving the beauty of spires.

We are not jugglers. Planes fall and leaves too and nothing that crashes or lands without sound gets repaired. Our ankles have sight of the horizon of small endings. We look forward to more as we leave more behind.

When my mother was dying, she asked, "Will I live?" I remember the silence as she turned from our silence to make herself ready, the quiet of an afternoon in a room where light and sound were present but respectful. I remember the quiet later that day as we stood alone with her. Absent at last, she withdrew with a tact saved for endings.

Please save me from all that I know must follow. Please give me a book or a song or a look that means less.

Commentary

"Singular" is a poem from *Here*, a 2014 collection in which I tried to find a way in the prose poem to move subject matter away from the "fabulous or fantastic toward available moments of observation and commentary."

I wanted to write prose poems more open and nimble in movement. I hoped to construct poems of very long and short lines, allowing the terrain to change sentence to sentence, syntax as topography, and within the poem, I wanted to allow for an observant voice to range over a number of experiences, reflections and realizations: to take in the inner and the tangible world was the goal.

As the poem progresses, a series of general and particular observations create a narrative in the first person plural, a "community voice," speaking of human agency in areas from religion to nature to friendship to love to death. The poem culminates in the narrator, reliving the death of her mother, making a plea for less meaning, a "way out" through language of what life holds. How we measure language to observe our sorrows and their passing is the culmination of the poem. To take in the moment's complexity and provide lucidity and range is the hope of the poem.

Unlike my earlier work, the voice is not meant to entertain or to confuse. Rather, it is a field in which feeling and voice explore their limits and fields of permission.

Laura Chester

Meteor Showers Purge the Indian summer sky, while boys lie down, sulfur spent, in the middle of midnight cornfields, shorn, to watch for sudden stars, to see some birthday being born. Their mother now remembers well that perfect face of infancy, falling into her fallen arms, pleading with her to re-turn. She hums. She waits for the proper blow to strike her rocking chair with sense. *What knocks?* She isn't a mother like other ones are. But sings as she canters through the wood, baroque tunes that feel of meadow and fox hedges, French horns. No leaves left. And life too dear. Babe in the arms of memory, sears like a shooting star. She should have a blaze on her forehead, to erase her bent—the provocative rip. A modest impulse, high noon. November plainly provides, visibility, (naked, stripped, cold). The heavens too will open and speak in the language of lasting iron and rose.

Commentary

Attempting to explain a prose poem is a bit like trying to dissect a flower—you end up with petals all over the floor. Where is the beauty of the blossom then? More importantly, the impulse behind the prose-poem form, for me, is being given free rein. Without the confines of line length or normal narrative, it is more like somnambulistic writing done in childhood's cuneiform code, where meaning is secondary, and what matters most is unveiling some hidden aspect, some profound, shared secret. This pact between writer and the page taps into the semi-conscious linking of the twilight reverie, what we go to sleep on, the prickling of memory, of audial and surface phenomenon, while couched in a sensate, natural landscape full of smells, textures, temperatures.

As Marcel Proust wrote: "Our vanity, our passions, our spirit of imitation, our abstract intelligence, our habits have long been at work, and it is the task of art to undo this work of theirs, making us travel back in the direction from which we have come to the depth where what has really existed lies unknown within us." What he describes might be something too primal to utter in plain prose, so the prose poem wears its disguise as if to dazzle as it disrobes. But it is also like stumbling upon a peephole focused onto the forbidden—the shock of seeing, hardly understanding, yet moved by the vision, pulled by an undertow that both rewards and threatens.

In reduction, for me, the above selection shines a light on the struggle between maternal love and a need for liberation from those demands, the conflict between nurturing and the raw power of sexuality embodied in the merging of woman and horse. Escape, versus comfort. The deep woods versus a steady rocking chair. And then there is the guilt and recrimination this choice carries with it—Should she be struck down? Should she be marked with a blaze on her forehead?

One phrase that stands out for me is—*What knocks?* What indeed! Death knocks, knocks at the door daily, as a reminder that it is always there, waiting. And does one's choice between safety and danger bring one closer to that knocking, to living fully while you have the chance?

Still, I wonder—am I compromising the prose poem by offering explanations? For an explanation seems to nip the beauty of the blossom in the bud. *Just allow that flower to break its sheath of ice, and warming, bloom in brightness. No one has to take it. Nothing to be said. Let it open toward the hills, the higher hills. Let it be the song on which you rise, even as the snow descends and absence animates the landscape, even at this time of darkness—Sing, for tomorrow will amaze us, as the constellation rides, and moonlight doubles in the heart of the beholder, balancing the curving slopes of white.*

The boys in the shorn field are freed from protection, abandoned to witness the heavens on a night of revelation, while the writer/rider rushes toward the power and tenderness of the word—

Lasting iron and rose. You tell me.

Kim Chinquee

Milk

Lilacs, cows, a lane between fields. Climbing on the stone pile. The smell of hay. Picking from the garden. Wintertime, the rain freezing on that garden, leaving an ice patch for your sister and you to skate on. The basketball hoop, right there by the silo. The machine shed, going there anytime you wanted and sitting on a tractor. When little, your mom claimed you had a fascination for the oil patches that your dad left. You'd sit there, the feel of it. At the end of the lane was a creek, and you could put your feet in, feeling the current, cold, and the water was so clear that you could spot the minnows. Sent by your mother, picking wild asparagus from the ditch along the road that had your name, your very same last name, which you were always proud of. Your ancestors made that road. They came from Germany and farmed there. Baling, lifting the bales, feeling the burn in your muscles, knowing about work. Getting up early, knowing calves were hungry, that they depended on you. You'd put that scoop into the bucket, mixing it with water, how the formula dissolved by the motion of your hand, how you mixed it until liquid, how you'd put the pail under these babies' noses, watching them slurp and suck to the bottom. How the new ones didn't know what to do. How your father had taught you how to teach them. Climbing the ladder to the hayloft with your sister. How the cats you didn't know scattered, how you'd look into the straw mounds, curious of the holes, how you'd come in with your flashlights, seeing those same cats giving birth there, with one thing in succession, those little creatures small as thumbs, slimy with their eyes closed, their mother licking them, your sister and you these big invaders with no rights to anything but a desire to know. Didn't matter that your father stripped you there more than once and slapped you, teaching you a lesson, a lesson, the lesson of the hayloft, of restraint, that restraint you learned so well, to not laugh nor cry: to not complain nor ask about anything. That hayloft, that bridge that you would walk across to take a bale to feed the heifers, that not being your desire, but your job, a way of survival as to not hear that yelling, how that one board was so wobbly and the hay bale was so heavy, how you'd just look ahead, never down, smelling the manure, and picturing those heifers, figuring they had to be hungry and how a growling stomach of your own was never a worry, how you knew there was abundance, how those same calves/heifer/cows/whatever you have fed being right there in the freezer, down to the heart and tongue and tail. How you ate them without pleasure. Eat, eat, eat, say the voices of your father, your mother just sitting there, getting fat and complaining about it though you never see her eating anything. How, you resorted to the garden, watching the corn sprout with the rain, picking a pod, popping a pea. You'd pluck the weeds. Your mother hoed and pushed her fancy tiller, taking breaks and sweating and saying what a hard job it is to keep a garden proper. You'd sit upright at the table, and then later, you would capture a tomato or a green bean, eating it raw and whole. You'd probably have to sneak it. You'd take it to the creek. You'd sit there with your feet, the current, cold. You'd close your eyes and bite. You'd taste, sweet juice, letting it drip.

Commentary

I wrote this piece in 2010. It was published in 2015 by *Cream City Review* under the title "Eat Your Plate." I mostly work from prompt words—since 2002, I've been hosting an online writing group called HotPants in Francis Ford Coppola's website *Zoetrope,* in a private office. Most days I'll post five prompt words (and lately a first-sentence prompt), and the group members post work and provide feedback. (We are currently on word set 3,682). I went back to see what the prompt words were for this. Alas, I didn't use any prompts, which surprised me, as that's how most of my work comes about. And it's fascinating to see what can come out with a varying set of prompts. I think, at this time, I was writing a lot about the farm where I grew up, and that propelled this piece. And I used my sensual memories from which to build.

In deciding on which piece to include for this anthology, I studied a lot of my work. I guess I'm mostly considered a "flash fiction" writer. "Milk" feels more like a prose poem to me, as it focuses more on language and tone and rhythm, and that, imo, is its momentum. Also, when looking at more of the defined terms of the forms, I like to rely on Michael Benedikt's definition of the prose poem. He says that it is characterized by a (1) reliance on the unconscious, (2) the use of everyday speech, (3) a visionary thrust, (4) a certain humor, and (5) a hopeful skepticism, whereas James Thomas, Denise Thomas, and Tom Hazuka, in their 1992 anthology *Flash Fiction,* were the first to define flash fiction as "a story of about 750 words, or a story that could fit onto two facing pages of a typical digest-size literary magazine; a story that is likely to include all those same elements of longer fiction, such as point-of-view, character, voice, setting, structure, and so on."

The process of writing prose poetry, to me, relies more on language, more on the thrust that Benedikt mentions, whereas writing fiction involves more of a momentum of plot. Though to me, the boundaries are never always clear, and that's part of the joy of it.

Brian Clements

Dream Letter

for Joe Ahearn

The earliest dream I remember: I'm running ahead of the devil, his pitchfork within reach of my ass, tail whipping the air, skin red as roasted peppers, eyebrows evilly arched. When I turn to look at him, the landscape rolls by in black and white B-movie panorama. He's coming closer, and when I turn back to look where I'm going, I smack face-first into a telephone pole. Then nothing. After the fact, I imagine my legs and arms stretched out in front, the pole holding my body there unnaturally long as the stars and birds and sparks fly around my head. But that's not in the dream. There is nothing; the dream ends without me.

Several times I've dreamt that I and an accomplice have buried a body behind a broken-down shed, or maybe in the woods. The accomplice is always whoever I love. Someone has found us out. We have to move the body. I don't know how we end up.

In the last dream I remember, I'm at a workshop of writers in a provincial Italian town. Cobblestone streets wind uphill through stone houses. I dorm with a few young writers and William S. Burroughs. When the others sleep, I steal Burroughs's manuscript and sneak out through the window, run down alleys, stir sleeping cats, avoid the cops in their little beeping Italian cars. I escape through a dumpster.

I don't believe in psychoanalysis, but I do believe in need. Sometimes I sit on my porch and watch the women gathered at the pool adjust their bodies and the fabrics and oils covering their bodies in the sun. I watch the men peeking out the corners of their eyes. In the evenings

I sometimes inspect my neighbors' windows, see shadows stretching and bending. Between blinds I sometimes glimpse a shoulder, a knee, unnamed flesh pressed into a pillow or crossed over other shapeless flesh. A woman downstairs sleeps with the lights on. I think she dreams of birds in the limbs above her, their eyes twitching in every direction on both sides of their heads.

Lately, I don't remember my dreams. I want to know what happens when they get lost. How does the mind adjust? When a friend dies of cancer, what happens to the other friends? I have friends I haven't spoken to in years. I remember their general shapes, but their faces bleed into the background. There is a picture on my wall of Burroughs standing in the jungle staring out the side of the frame, his gaze distant, as if watching language fade out of sight, his mouth agape, speechless. I imagine he's in Mexico, though it's probably Africa, and it's probably his wife he's watching become less and less visible.

My friend Michelle likes to ask, "Which do you prefer—coming or going?" which leaves out the possibility of being there. When I try to place myself in the past, I always picture the play of light on the trees, which stands for everything else. I don't believe in everything, but the poem is smaller than the world. Between them, the dream dreams. None of its people the people we know, nothing in it like what we do.

Commentary

I returned to this poem recently thinking that it had been my first prose poem, but as I re-read it I realized that it hadn't. A few years earlier I had been experimenting with one-sentence-per-paragraph things that I didn't know to call prose poems; I was steered away from that path by a couple of mentors in grad school. I didn't yet have the sense to recognize what promised to be a rich vein for me in the face of disapproval from fairly conservative authority.

It took me a few years after grad school to publish my first book, and this poem was in that book. In the interim, I had grown weary of the Creative Writing Publication Game and realized that I had been writing into the expectations of others, rather than pursuing what was useful to my own exploration. With a group of poets in Dallas that included Joe Ahearn and others, we started making and sharing poems using Oulipo and other operational composition strategies. We called ourselves Synthetics, collecting language from the world and weaving the bits and pieces together into poems and collages. It was during that community collaboration of a few years that most of the prose poems in my books *And How to End It* and *Jargon* were written.

But this poem predated the Synthetic poems we made by a few years. I had known Joe Ahearn for going on ten years at this point, and he had written a letter poem to me around the time that I moved back to Dallas from Binghamton, called "Belly Letter." "Dream Letter" was my response to his prose poem, so I was thinking of it more as a letter poem than as a prose poem per se. But in retrospect I think it highly unlikely that I ever would have returned to the prose poem with the Synthetic poets if it weren't for this exchange of poems with Joe. I then went through a period of about six years where I wrote prose poems exclusively.

Both Joe and I were tutored by the great poet and teacher Jack Myers—I was Jack's student as an undergrad, and Joe knew Jack through a community poets group through which Jack had introduced Joe and me. So in a very practical way Jack was the connection between Joe and me, but I also sense Jack in the background of this poem; in some sense, a lot of the work of my writing has been a conversation with Jack, a conversation with Joe about my conversation with Jack, a conversation with Oulipo and Surrealism and O'Hara and Ashbery and America about one of the questions that lay at the center of Jack's work throughout his life: am I being good?

I left Dallas in 2004 to move with my family to Newtown, CT, where in 2012 my wife Abbey survived the shooting (she was not shot).

For about 18 months after the shooting, I was unable to write poems of any kind (by which I mean in no way whatsoever to compare that problem to the murder of a loved one, especially a child). I am sure that part of the reason I was unable to write poems was because being good now meant engaging politically in the real world in a way I had never been called upon to do in the past. But I had no choice; being good now meant working on gun violence, not writing poems. I was not able to return to writing poems until I was able to find a way to make writing poems and being good in this new context the same thing. I needed to insert myself into a different conversation.

The idea of writing as part of a conversation will be new to no one reading this. But thinking about this poem and about Joe and Jack and about the Synthetics and the Dallas Poets Community and about grad school and about *The Prose Poem: An International Journal* and about *Sentence: A Journal of Prose Poetics* and about the national gun violence prevention community has reminded me that we are the relationships we cultivate; we are the conversations we continue for days, for months, some 25 years later. So I'm not talking here so much about the poem I've selected, but about the world of the poem, the community of the poem, which is so much more important than the poem itself.

Peter Conners

A Man Learns To Fly

In his younger years his father had toted him out to the bird feeder. It was brown, bent, speckled with white droppings—angled against all seasons. No mix was sufficient to keep the lesser birds away: Old bruise-colored grackles arrived on the scene. Meager starlings. Rusty female cardinals. At each new mix, elated, they waited, but the loveliest of feathered winds never blew their way. And so the father taught him to love the ugly ones. Named them after earls and dukes, invested them with flight patterns to shame the baldest of eagles.

In the boy's front yard, truly, the meek had inherited the earth.

Such is the ornithology of family.

A boy flew away one morning to return a man to find his father turned to ash beside a bag of grainy seeds. And this note: *Help me to fly.*

Commentary

This poem was written shortly after the birth of my first son. Whitman was born 12 days before 9/11 and the weeks around his birth were filled with a mixture of elation and anxiety about the future. Thanks to a flexible schedule, I was fortunate to be able to spend a lot of time with my newborn son. Once he was strong enough, we passed many weekdays with him strapped to my chest, walking to various parks and shops around our neighborhood and communicating (communing) with each other in a newly discovered language. At home, there was a large window overlooking a tiny, patchy front lawn, with, of course, a "brown, bent" bird feeder "speckled with white droppings." We'd sit on the couch in front of that window and watch the birds. They were not unique as far as species go, but they were miraculous—they were birds! They flew! They pecked at seeds and each other and they were the first birds that Whitman had witnessed and the first birds I experienced with Whitman. There we were: father and son, post-9/11 America, watching these "meager" birds visit our feeder, waiting inside some impossible bubble that could never last and will never end. That moment of time is "A Man Learns to Fly." I don't know what else I can do. I don't know what else I can say.

Jon Davis

The Bait

This is not an elegy because the world is full of elegies and I am tired of consoling and being consoled. Because consolation is unsatisfying and even tenderness can do nothing to stop this loss, this dying, this viciousness among men.

And god just complicates, offering justice like the cracker I place on this mouse trap. Then frantic mouse hands pushing against the metal bar, kicking and bucking, the fall from the shelf, more kicking, one eye bulging, lips lifted and the little yellowed teeth clamped on the small crumb of goodness that was not goodness but something alluring and, finally, dumb—without equivalent in the human world. Just food he couldn't have.

My food and what that means in the scale of human affairs. I didn't want to listen to this mouse scrabbling among the graham crackers, chewing into the can of grease, leaving a trail of greasy, orange, rice-like shits in the cabinet under the sink. I didn't want to clean those up every morning; I didn't want to be awakened in the night.

I set the trap; the trap smashed his skull; he kicked a while and he died. I tossed him, trap and all, into the dunes. But I was saying something about god and justice. I was saying this is not an elegy and why. Because pain is the skin we wear? Because joy is that skin also?

Because ... look: I had a brother and he died. I didn't cause it; I couldn't stop it. He got on his motorcycle and rode away. A car turned in front of him and that began his dying. How terrible for everyone involved. Do I sound bitter? I felt the usual guilts: Did I love him enough. Did I show it.

It happened eleven years ago and what I remember: Looking out at the lawn, September and a breeze; watching him ride—flash of red gas tank, brown leather jacket; the sound of the bike; what we said, which I recall as a kind of gesture, the sound of *what are you doing,* some dull rhythm and *see you later.*

The phone call. The drive to the hospital. I think 1 drove but I can't be sure. We drove the wrong way down a one-way street and I remember feeling responsible. I cried most of the time. I knew he was dying. My brother's girlfriend asked me *Why are you crying?* and I couldn't say or else I sobbed *It's bad I know it's bad.*

Then we were taken into a green room and told he was dead. I curled on a red plastic chair. My body disappeared or seemed to. I was looking for my brother; a nurse called me back: *Your family needs you.* I came back.

But why am I telling you this? Because I want you to love me? To pity me? To understand I've suffered and that excuses my deficiencies? To see how loss is loss and no elegy, no quiet talk late at night among loved ones who suddenly feel the inadequacy of their love and the expression of that love can take it away? Or give it back? Perhaps even loss is lost?

My brother is gone and the world, you, me, are not better for it. There was no goodness in his death. And there is none in this poem, eleven years later and still confused. An attempt, one might say, to come to terms with his death as if there were somewhere to come to, as if there were terms. But there is nowhere to come to; there are no terms. Just this spewing of words, this gesture neither therapy nor catharsis nor hopelessness nor consolation. Not elegy but a small crumb. An offering.

Commentary

I wrote "The Bait" in 1987 when I was Writing Program Coordinator at the Fine Arts Work Center in Provincetown. Bob Ross, a friend and a fellow at FAWC that year, had a computer. At some point that fall, he invited me to try his newfangled writing device. After a quick lesson in whatever primitive word processing program he was then using, I was off. I believe this was the second poem I wrote on the device. I remember being thrilled at the way I could feel my way into the poem, quickly deleting words, sentences, paragraphs, and reversing direction when I felt I'd gone astray (though what constituted "astray" is always a bit intuitive and mysterious, since to stray one must have a destination, and I never had one).

I'd been working with prose poems since reading and hearing, in 1984, the pieces that would make up the bulk of Robert Hass's *Human Wishes.* I'd published two prose poems in my first book, *Dangerous Amusements.* In some ways my movement toward the prose poem was a reaction to the often cramped, image-centered lyric of the 80's workshop and the hours-long discussions of line breaks, which always seemed to me like discussing color-choices on the *Titanic.* There was a bigger question to entertain: Will it float?

But the fact is every poem I wrote between 1988 and 1995 was written against something. Against the confines of the graduate poetry workshop. Against the one-page imagistic lyric. Against the line. Against the prohibition on abstraction. Against "craft" as an absolute term. Against, in this case, elegy. And against, in this case, (why not?) god.

But how did the poem happen? There's not much to say. I started at the top of the page and descended, downward to darkness, at breakneck speed. The speed let me write about my brother's death at all. Kept me from getting bogged down in the muck and mire of the subject. Kept me from landing on a hopeful illusion.

Although I'd been obsessively reading Gertrude Stein, Leslie Scalapino, Michael Palmer, and Lyn Hejinian, writers for whom connection is problematic, I remember having E. M. Forster's "Only connect!" and Frank O'Hara's essay "Personism" ("I realized I could use the telephone instead of writing the poem") in mind as I began composing. In fact, I was taking those suggestions so to heart that I included my actual phone number in the last line of the first draft.

A number of other voices were in my head: Jorie Graham's essay, "Some Notes on Silence": "Abstract diction … feels especially powerful to me because of its poignancy, the sense of desperation that informs it, the sense of a last avenue being resorted to, a last, bluntest tool." Charles Olson's "Projective Verse," and his command to "get on with it, keep moving, keep in, speed, the nerves, their speed, the perceptions, theirs, the acts, the split-second acts, the whole business, keep it moving as fast as you can, citizen." And also thinking, per Maximus, about making the poem on the page the event itself and not the record of the event.

The directness of the poem, which probably had its roots in Nicanor Parra's poems and Antonin Artaud's prose poems, still makes me uncomfortable, though that directness was required. "All this / Had to be imagined as an inevitable knowledge, / Required, as a necessity requires," as Wallace Stevens wrote in "The Plain Sense of Things," one of my favorite Stevens poems.

So: I wrote fast. I rewrote little. I lopped my phone number off, tinkered with word choice, and created the stanza/paragraph breaks. Though the poem has received more attention than all but one other poem I've written and has been used by priests and psychologists in grief-work, I don't often read it aloud. It's too direct, too close to the bone. It still throws me down a well and leaves me there a while in the dark.

Peter Davis

Hitler's Mustache: The Short Story

Important arrangements were to be made. The party would not plan itself. She sat on her square, black sofa, dreaming about the decorations and imagining the caterer and even some of the clothes her guests might be wearing. It made here happy to like this. But, soon enough, her grand hopes began to settle like soft snow on the warm floor of the situation. She didn't have much money. A. Would never get behind her on this. Her sister-in-law would drink too much and break her square, black heel and throw her purse in the swimming pool and fall asleep in a lawn chair. There were bills that needed to be paid now. If only she had never met mustache. If only he hadn't mustached her aunt in a furnace, or breaded her over and open mustache.

That evening while her husband and children ate the food she had carefully mustached for them, she got an idea. Perhaps, she thought, if I were to mistake something for mustache. It seemed perfect. It covered all the angles. A. would get behind it because he needed that mustache. Her sister-in-law would take care of the bills. The cold snow began to melt. As a metaphor for her mood the cold snow no longer made sense and began to drift upward, out of the story, out of the poem, existing only in the past, in another time, one that seemed much bleaker.

The next morning she packed the children's lunches and pressed A's shirt for him. After the kids were on the bus, and A. kissed her cheek and drove the Volkswagen down the long driveway, she fed the mustache and packed her baggage. She called the mustache. Put a not on the door for the mustache, and left, making sure she left the mustache slightly cracked so the mustache would be able to mustache the mustache.

The day was hot and by the time she reached the airport she was sweating through her shirt. She fanned herself with a mustache and nervously surveyed the situation. There were two guards near the mustache. Each mustache looked like it held a mustache. She ordered a cup of mustache from the mustache who worked behind the mustache.

Mustache knew that she couldn't mustache about this forever. She'd have to make up her mind mustache. She studied the mustache. She thought about all of the mustache in her mustache. All of the mustache and the mustache and the must ache and mustache. She thought about the mustaches when her mustache was put in mustache. She took one more mustache of mustache. She mustached. She mustached her mustache and with every mustache of her mustache, mustached.

Commentary

So, once upon a time, I started writing about Hitler's mustache, which to me represents the mystery that is always present, the anomaly, the question mark in the heart of every answer. Hitler's face is a universal symbol of evil, and yet it has that odd black square in the middle of it, an island of superfluous fashion on the sea of Hitler's otherwise efficiently cruel look. I just kept writing and writing about Hitler's mustache till it soon became a manuscript and, eventually, my first book of poems, aptly titled *Hitler's Mustache.* It was like I'd found a black, square trapdoor and I just fell in. Lots of the poems in the book took on already existing forms like the list, the memo, the sestina, the jingle, etc. till I finally got to this poem, the short story. These poems weren't exclusively about Hitler's actual mustache, but also about the actual words "Hitler's mustache." The word "mustache" became more and more prominent in my imagination. Whenever I was writing and I paused, considering what word to choose,

I began to choose the word "mustache" as a placeholder, so to speak. Soon I realized that this word had become a sort of fascist, running wild with power and trampling the words in my poems. It was as if the word "mustache," combined with the idea of Hitler's actual mustache, wanted to black out everything with its square, black implications. Of course, the sound of the word "mustache" is really quite a mouthful and funny and sad in its own way, just as Hitler's actual mustache was also funny and sad in its own way. So, in the end, what happens in this poem is a sort of microcosm of the fascist process. As the story proceeds, the word mustache becomes more frequent, more belligerent, till it is nearly every word. And if the poem went on much further than it does, "mustache" would soon become the only word in the poem.

Michel Delville

Marcel Duchamp

A thermometer and a cuttlefish bone with nothing in the mix from Montale. A cage filled with cubes stamped Made in France. Mannerisms in the absence of style. One day or another, the nominal sentence will eventually outskin ambient minimalism. *This makes it art.* The readymade neither deceives nor cheats. To the touch, the material remains constant. The strength of objects answers a new classicism, patient and monochrome. Then comes the opposite feat. Sugar hardens into diced metamorphic rocks' varicose faces. How many angels on the head of a pin? Speculation prevails through a kind of anorexic euphoria. The most stubborn among us will imagine the plumage of the absent bird.

Commentary

I am mainly a prose poet. What I do is write very short stories for people with a short attention spans, alongside very short essays for people who have no patience for full-length philosophical treatises.

"Marcel Duchamp" is taken from a collection of imaginary portraits of modern and contemporary artists ranging from Montaigne to Captain Beefheart. While some of these "prose poems and microessays" are grounded in the life and works of the artists, others were generated by a more personal, subjective, associational logic that pays tribute to the complex, whimsical and paradoxical legacy of Belgian Surrealism. More often than not, the works and artists considered here are seen through the lens of the conjunction of food and discourse, from a perspective that stresses the need to attend to the movements of a consciousness which is as visceral as it is cerebral.

Readers familiar with Duchamp's work will instantly understand that this poem is about Duchamp's ready-made *Why Not Sneeze Rose Sélavy?*—a bird cage containing marble cubes resembling sugar cubes, a thermometer and cuttlefish bone. They will pick up on (and hopefully prolong) the half-sketched reflections on the legacy of found art and ready-mades, which include thoughts about proto-minimalism and the dangers of the solidification of anti-art gestures into so many aesthetic mannerisms.

(Even) more astute (or "stubborn") readers might spot a reference to Eugenio Montale's *Cuttlefish Bones* in the opening sentence, a quote from Gertrude Stein's *Tender Buttons* ("*This makes it art*"), and a tribute to Duchamp's Mallarmean poetics (the "absent bird" echoes the "clear ice-flights that never flew away" of the 1887 poem "The Virgin, the Vivacious, and the Beautiful Present Day"). As for the sugar cubes hardening into marble, they can be elucidated in the light of the artist's pronouncement that the cage is "filled with sugar lumps … but the sugar lumps are made of marble and when you lift it, you are surprised by the unexpected weight. / The thermometer is to register the temperature of the marble" (Duchamp). One of the purposes of this block of prose is indeed to imagine how Duchamp's installation would *feel* if museum visitors were allowed to open the bird cage, hold it with one hand and reach for its contents with the other. Perhaps only by approaching Duchamp's installation through other senses than the sense of sight can one hope to resist the temptation of counting angels dancing on pinheads.

This close reading does not really tell us what a "prose poem" or a "microessay" is or is not, but it does convey a sense of how speculative thought can be used and, some will argue, abused in a format which simultaneously celebrates essayistic prose and undermines it, so to speak, from within. It is my hope that by resisting the syllogistic movement of descriptive prose, and by opting for a disjunctive and paratactic style while privileging free association over expository coherence, "Marcel Duchamp" multiplies, rather than reduces, the vectors of meaning generated by its object of study.

Chard deNiord

The Music

If fish are notes in the river then the song is never the same, even if the water is. Heraclitus was wrong. The current is motion is all. You touch a dancer as she pirouettes and she's still the same dancer. So there is a song that never gets played because the fish are always swimming in a way that rejects notation? If they stopped where they are right now would they configure a song? Are they swimming, therefore, forever toward a melody? If so, you could say then that any song is the prescient catch of a school of fish at various depths, a quick and natural analogue for composition, the trout song, the bass song, the perch song. But the mind is the antinomy of a river, says Mr. Tsu. It is not the song beneath the surface that the fish suggest, for those songs never exist in time, but the fixed clear notes above the surface that are pinned to a sheet, on bars. The music we hear is played by musicians who have learned the difference between an idea and a score. So, Kepler was wrong also about the spheres, and Scriabin about the spectrum, and David about the hills. None of these things contain music. Only the mind thinks they do. Only the mind would ruin their silence with a symphony.

Commentary

I wrote this prose poem as a metaphysical rumination after thinking about Kepler's "music of the spheres" or *Harmonices Mundi.* But instead of thinking about heavenly bodies as notes, I envisioned fish as notes. This image initially inspired me to think about music as an animated flow of musical notations rather than as a fixed score. But then I wondered, for reasons I can't recall, just what Lao-Tzu might say about the notion of fish embodying notes, which prompted me, in turn, to think about the difference between my poetic idea of piscatory notes and actual notes. I knew there were precedents for such thinking about music in Scriabin's vision of notes as colors and David's apprehension of music as silence itself (Psalm 19), but I didn't want to leave it at that. I wanted to distinguish between the mystical music of the imagination—those mysterious melodies one hears with her third, interior ear, whether it be in mathematical, synesthetical, or imagistic ways, as in my case—and actual composed music that interrupts the silence in which meta-music resides inherently as the first music any composer hears in mere things themselves before composing their scores.

Karen Donovan

Spirits

Alembic.
a **Head;** *b* **Cucurbit;** *c* **Receiver;** *d* **Lamp.**

Your substance, such as it is, in liquid solution subjected to direct heat sufficient to cause a rolling boil, will begin to come apart into its constituent elements. What is heaviest will settle into layers like tree rings of mud on the floor of a thousand-year flood plain and glue itself to your bones. That afternoon, the lab assistants will have trouble scraping it off the bottom of the glass and will enjoy themselves cursing you for your ponderous carboniferous rationality. What is lightest will fly up, spiraling heavenward as if released from the laws of gravity and cosmological constants, only to instantly bump their heads on the ceiling tiles. Like bees trying to get out of a room by aiming the only way they know how, up, they collect there as a golden atmosphere, an exhalation, and when they tire they deliquesce like breath condensing on a mirror, like pale exhaust exiting a warm body on a cold morning.

Before long, there's an entire cupful. You do not escape but forget what you were before, which is almost the same thing.

Commentary

Stack up about ten Chromebooks, throw on an embossed clothbound cover, and you have roughly the dimensions and weight of the 1925 *Webster's New International Dictionary of the English Language.* There it sits on my bookstand—a fat, heavy, and glorious tome originally owned by my grandfather Raymond. Open it anywhere and disappear into its thicket of language. It contains, among other wonders, a pronouncing gazetteer and biographical dictionary and a color plate showing turn-of-the-century yacht club flags of the U.S. and Canada. The fore-edge is thoughtfully tabbed to take you easily to the As or the Ps or the Qs.

As a poet, I have always loved dictionaries. But what most captivated me about this one was the beautiful engravings. Who makes dictionaries like this anymore? It is stuffed with weirdly, wizardly alchemical drawings of plants, animals, insects, tools, weapons, architecture, and archaic scientific gizmos. I picked dozens of illustrations from the A section. My method was thus: every night when I got home from work I would sit down, choose a picture that called out to me, and write a short response—a tiny essay, a flash memoir, a fable, a fragment, a list, an instruction, a song, a prayer, a prose poem, whatever seemed right. Certainly, this was plain old ekphrasis, writing about art, but it was also something else. I began to feel as though I was working out definitions for the engravings. I was participating in a prison revolt by the pictures. They were going to break free from denotation entirely, and I was just the doorway.

Denise Duhamel

Scalding Cauldron

Calling all Cosmic, Counterclock-Wise, Crackpot Crones who denounce docility, doublethink, and the domains of dummies. Our dragon eyes open, we exalt emotion, elixirs, and all elemental spirits. Our Foremothers forecasted the forests would be finished off, that feeble fembots would fall for fabricated fables. And here we are—at the future.

From the fortress of our fury, we begin this gyromancy (a practice in which a poet/witch seeks divination from a walk around the alphabet, taking note of the letters upon which she stumbles). Calling all Goddesses and Goofballs, Glamorous Grammarians, Giggling Gaggles of Geniuses, Gorgons and Gossips, Gyno-centric Gals, Heathens, Harpies, and Hags to come along and make this hexing hike. In this Intercourse of Individual Incarnations, may we intervene and influence junkies (ourselves?) addicted to joyless joists and other junk. On this journey, may we kick-start Kinship, put the kibosh on lecherous leeches and their laws, embrace the labyrinth of our lunacy, smash our mirrors.

May we maze our way through amazement, moon-wise, naming and renaming what has been misnamed. Calling all Nags and Nag-gnostics, Nag-noteworthy Nixes, and Nymphs. Calling all Outsiders, Ogres, those who check "Other," those from Otherworldly places, those Overlooked, and Old Maid Outercourse Pilgrims. Together we will chant, *Piss off—passive voice.* (A woman was not raped. Someone raped a woman.)

Calling all Pagans, Pixies, Prideful Prudes, Philosophers, Queens, and Quacks to rage and reverse, writing our Recourse to remember and reinvent our very syntax/sin-tax. Let's speckle the cracks with our sparkling cackles. Let's scold and scald. Let's *be* Skalds—poets who write of heroic deeds. Calling all Sisters, Sinners, Spinsters, Shrewd Shrews, Seers and Self-Realized Sirens. Calling all Soothsayers and Sinister Sprites, Shape-shifters and Separatists who cast spells. Take a trek through this untidy alphabet. There will be toads and tidal time, the third ear and third eye. Traverse through unconventionality, where virtue and vice collide. Virgins and Vixens may experience vertigo, new to such wanderlust/wonderlust in this Wickedary. XX for kisses, XX for dead cartoon eyes. How we yearn at this zero hour.

(Where did you trip? Where did you fall? Please plan your augury accordingly.)

Our scalding cauldron is an abecedarian aquarium, boundless bubbles be-musing and be-monstering. We needn't stay one course: Recourse/Shulie Firestone; Intercourse/Andrea Dworkin; or Outercourse/Mary Daly, of course.

Commentary

This prose poem is the title-ish poem from my latest book *Scald.* It owes quite a bit to Mary Daly's 1987 feminist classic *Websters' First New Intergalactic Wickedary of the English Language.* Daly's book is indeed a witchy dictionary, reclaiming and/or redefining language that is often used against women. I was inspired to take a romp through Daly's definitions, some thirty years later, using an abecedarian prose block. I started with the letter "C" which alludes to cunt, possibly the most egregious of words used to denigrate a woman. I was interested in Daly's decision to write "gynomorphically" and see this poem as a rallying cry to embrace the English language while also being aware of its socio-political pitfalls. The prose poem is an invitation to unconventional thinkers, so it was fun for me to begin with "Calling all …" as a sort of ethical Pied Piper.

"Scalding Cauldron" uses the imperative voice, demanding that the reader follow. Much of the chutzpah of second wave feminism was built on argument and metaphor, just as a poem is built. The prose poem, in particular, is bold in its claims and follows a logic all its own. If poetry can exist in prose, actualized women can exist in language that is seemingly used against them. Poetry and prose are not opposites. Neither are men and women. The prose poem collapses what we think of as binary and instead invites unity. While women are always told they are implicitly included in mankind, isn't it truer that men are included in womankind? Womankind actually contains the word "man." The prose poem is a space in which all this can be explored—Prideful Prudes and Sinners can coexist; fembots and Hags can come together. Some purists still argue that the prose poem does not exist, just as some argue feminism cannot save us. I end the poem giving props to Shulie Firestone and Andrea Dworkin, two radicals very different from Daly. I hope the three live on in contentment gathered around the cauldron.

Jamey Dunham

Trickster at the Free Clinic

The sweet stench of urine and a hypo for every junkie. The circus is in town and Coyote is a kid again. Gone are the days of cotton candy and popcorn, Italians flung to the sawdust. Yet the clowns remain, their numbers swelling as they stream from the men's room as if from a tiny car. In the waiting area an addict climbs onto his seat and prepares for his next dive. He steadies himself against the magazine rack and peers down at the linoleum rippling below. The show has begun and Coyote grabs a seat up front beside an especially gruesome leper. "Pardon me, but could you lend me a hand?" "Mind if I steal your ear for a moment?" "Hey Buddy, is that your dick on the floor?" Coyote enjoying the show, taking in all the sights. The freaks are all sufficiently freakish, though Coyote has a hard time telling the bearded lady from the fat lady as both are bearded and morbidly obese. A nurse emerges from behind a curtain to address the crowd. "Schwebel?" she asks. "Schwebel?" "Two over here," calls Coyote, passing a ten down the row. A page booms out over the loud speaker, "Doctor Ahmad, paging Doctor Ahmad. Doctor Ahmad to obstetrics." Coyote takes his cue and leaps into the spotlight. Coyote spectator no more. Coyote ringmaster, Coyote top hat of the big top working the crowd into a frenzy. "Ladies and Gentleman, the moment you've been waiting for has finally arrived," he announces to the bruised and the bleeding. Coyote splashes through the swinging doors of the delivery ward nearly knocking over a nurse. He turns to face the crowd, bows low at the waist then tears open the medical curtains theatrically. "Ladies and gentleman … behold the greatest show on earth!"

Commentary

I suspect I was first drawn to write "Trickster" poems for many of the same reasons I was originally attracted to the prose poem itself. Like the shape-shifting character of Coyote, the prose poem has always occupied a precarious position in the literary landscape. With one foot in myth and the other groping for a toehold in truth, the poems straddle such an existential divide they seem to lose track of their feet altogether and appear instead as a mysterious crotch spread across the horizon. And just as the sight of celestial genitalia would likely stir alternating waves of curiosity and horror, arousal and disgust, so too has the prose poem been simultaneously embraced and disparaged to the point of near dismissal. Add to that the additional concerns of cultural insensitivity and appropriation and you really can't help but wonder why anyone would unlatch the gate and wander into these woods unless it be for the lure of danger itself.

Nearly every culture has some example of the Trickster archetype; from the Norse god Loki, to the clever Kitsune of Japan. The character of Coyote, prevalent in the trickster tales of many western Native American tribes, seemed a particularly good fit for my own aesthetic sensibilities and poetic pursuits. In my childhood, it was the Wile E. Coyote of Saturday morning cartoons who captivated me with his endlessly inventive, if not ill-fated, exploits. Those Looney Toons episodes were also a perfect introduction to the surreal and skewed world my own prose poems would later inhabit. Though the medium of the cartoon might have been relegated to the province of children, it was impossible to miss the adult themes and dark humor that pervaded them. Just as with Michaux's character Plume, written years earlier, the world glimpsed in those cartoons was, at once, fantastically absurd and brutally relatable.

Even the actual coyote itself (*Canis latrans*) is a perfect metaphor for the prose poem. Simultaneously reviled and respected, the coyote of my current suburban existence continues to occupy a special place in the public imagination. With an outward appearance somewhere between dog and wolf, the coyote seems to exist in two worlds at once: the civilized and the wild. Its very existence in our otherwise sterile neighborhoods seems to upend convention and reassert possibility. It may strew garbage across your front lawn or it may stare into your soul before disappearing behind a strip mall. It may serenade you on a warm summer night or it may make off with your neighbor's cat. Like a good prose poem, it's a survivor, continually skirting the boundaries of convention and exploiting the expectations of anyone foolish enough to get too comfortable.

Stuart Dybek

Inland Sea

Horizon, a clothesline strung between crabapples. The forgotten dress, that far away, bleached invisible by a succession of summer days until a thunderstorm drenches it blue again, as it is now, and despite the distance, the foam of raindrops at its hem sparkles just before the wind lifts it into a wave that breaks against the man framed in a farmhouse doorway.

Commentary

The prose poem has always been a laboratory of prose rhythm for me. The visual effect of reducing the length of a piece of prose on a page seems to heighten the aural effects of prose, and to encourage the writer to explore the unscannable music of simultaneity along the staff of a sentence. Is it that the tighter visual dimensions simply slow down reading? Perhaps in a poem in prose the sound of the interplay of sentences gains back in subtlety some of what it loses in "songfullnesse" in giving up the interplay of sentence rhythm with the beat of line. The effect crosses genre; I'm consciously aware of it in certain fictions such as those vignettes in Hemingway's *in our time* where his youthful experiments with brevity, understatement, tone, and repetition well might have been called minimalism had the term been coined back in 1924. Although they can coexist in the same piece, brevity and compression are, of course, not the same thing. Poetry, whether in verse or prose, is written with the intention (and hope) that it can be read more than once. For me, it's compression rather than obscurity that encourages rereading. I love aphorisms and have long admired Paul Valery's *What is more mysterious than clarity?*

Russell Edson

The Tunnel

I went tunneling into the earth ...

My wife and I going through an inventory of reasons, found nothing sufficient to the labor.

Still, she allowed, as I, that a direction once started, as if desire, and the desire to be desired, were mutually igniting, drew the traveler to its end without explainable reason ...

Yet, does not the southern direction in extreme horizon look to the north, even as that of the north, finding the apex of its final arc, nod wearily south...?

So I went tunneling into the earth, through darkness that penetration only makes darker, faithful to the idea of light, said always to be at the end of tunnels; perhaps not yet lit, but in the universe moving in rendezvous, thus to shimmer under the last shovelful of earth ...

Commentary

Looking at this piece again after a long time, it does seem somewhat overly punctuated and full of clauses, as if it has longed another way than sentences and paragraphs. But it is the blah blah and hiss of prose since having first met literature in company of Dick and Jane that holds me in mystery. Dick and Jane, they had a dog named Spot.

I went tunneling into the earth ... For what? Gold? To make a grave? Or simply to find a more direct route to China? So-called deep meanings bore me. They're so common as to run in the streets like tears. One assumes meaning even if one is looking the other way as the work unfolds. Language is meaning without one's having to dig a tunnel for it. I had no idea what the speaker would do with his first line. But as the piece continued it seemed to be making fairly good sense, even if its speaker, claiming to be tunneling into darkness expecting light, didn't. The contradiction between the keys of one's keyboard and what they can type make for a kind of ticklish fun, jellifying one's brain into shimmering delight.

But, as I look at the piece again, though short, it moves with obsessive detail in its back and forthness, like a contract being drawn between reality and paranoia, that finally resolves itself in the cliché about the light at the end of tunnels. Incidentally, I like writing soliloquies when possible; they're easier than having to write two voices. And of course it's always a piece of luck to find a cliché that fits one's work. The cliché is greatly underrated, when, in fact, it's a valuable tool of understanding: acting as a shorthand that frees the writer from having to do too much on his own. After about fifteen minutes one wants to try something else. As I say, writing is ticklish fun, but too much tickling makes me nervous. This is why the prose poem is a good device for the nervous writer. Ideally, prose poems are short, which allows the writer to move from piece to piece rather quickly. But the best part is that so little is expected of the prose poem that the writer doesn't really have to push himself too hard, or to write at all if he just happens not to be in the mood. "The Tunnel" at the time just happened to fit my mood. And as I read through it again, it still does. All a writer really needs is some intuition, and a fair memory for clichés, and the desire to make something out of almost nothing at all. For no matter the content or nature of a work, there is the grand abstraction beyond the self. The *shape* of thought, the impersonal music of silence hovering over every page like a ghost emptied from a land of shadows …

Beth Ann Fennelly

What I Think about When Someone Uses "PUSSY" as a Synonym for "WEAK"

At the deepest part of the deepest part, I rocked shut like a stone. I'd climbed as far inside me as I could. Everything else had fallen away. Midwife, husband, bedroom, world: quaint concepts. My eyes were clamshells. My ears were clapped shut by the palms of the dead. My throat was stoppered with bees. I was the fox caught in the trap, and I was the trap. Chewing off a leg would have been easier than what I now required of myself. I understood I was alone in it. I understood I would come back from there with the baby, or I wouldn't come back at all. I was beyond the ministrations of loved ones. I was beyond the grasp of men. Even their prayers couldn't penetrate me. The pain was such that I made peace with that. I did not fear death. Fear was an emotion, and pain had scalded away all emotions. I chose. In order to come back with the baby, I had to tear it out at the root. Understand, I did this without the aid of my hands.

Commentary

A few years back, I was in the audience at a reading series in a hipster bar when a young man stepped to the microphone to introduce the next writer. The writer had apparently been a mentor to the young man, who spoke about the writer's work and influence, becoming emotional. All this seemed to me rather charming, but not to the young man; "I can't believe I'm up here crying like a pussy," he said.

In the days that followed, I kept thinking about and around that sentence. What troubled me? Not that he'd sworn—I can swear like a truck driver—just ask the witnesses of my IKEA baby crib assembly. No, my rejection of his statement is not because "pussy" is vulgar but because it's a bad metaphor—how did that strong part of a woman's strong body become co-opted as symbol for weakness? This could not be. I picked up my pen.

I'll mention that this piece is in my book, *Heating & Cooling: 52 Micro-Memoirs.* I came up with the term "micro-memoirs" to indicate I was writing small, true stories. I didn't want to use the term "poetry" because I'd grown wary of my "speaker," my mask; I wanted to claim my experiences as my own. Further, I didn't call the pieces "prose poems" because most of them weren't. The piece above is an exception, composed with a poet's sensibility—including the rhythms of poetry, its repetitions and syntax and metaphorical leaps.

Let me think through the differences between the line versus the sentence, a distinction that would seem dainty to those who aren't obsessed with words, who assume lines are chopped-up sentences. But those of us who *are* obsessed with words know the distinction changes not only how but what we write. After all, if lines were merely chopped-up sentences, and line breaks merely visual, we could delete them with no change to the material. But when losing the line break, we lose the white space that shapes the way we process meaning. Line breaks provide a rest, so the words on either side of the rest can require more effort in the processing of lyricism, tropes, syntax, and sound. These resting places—like stair landings in a walk-up—interrupt the exertion with a breather (literally), and so give us the strength to keep climbing. Without them, too much is demanded of us, so our absorption is hindered.

The poetic line also affects the reader because it highlights the artfulness and artifice of the experience of reading, as opposed to the sentence, which distracts us from it. The line, followed by its white space, metes out comprehension, followed by its disruption. The power play of the line break is that of withholding. We're never unaware that our experience is being modulated by another as we follow the choreographer's orders to leap and rest, leap and rest. This is fundamentally different than how prose pours itself into the vase of the page. *Here,* says the line, *Now we are here. Now we are here.* But *everywhere,* says the sentence.

You are everywhere and nowhere. The sentence is always pointing outside of itself. This is what Cole Swenson means, I believe, when she writes "Prose exists somewhere other than the page."

Gerald Fleming

Crucifixion, Kinetic

Often, the scene depicted as tranquil—fait accompli, three men in their proper places, on crosses, assorted provokers and grievers below, sky leaden, sense overall not meat but vegetal, varnished, *tableau.*

Let's say it did occur.

Then: *cross?* This planed and surfaced lumber in pictures we knew long ago—in Giotto, Raphael, even Goya?

No. Rough spar. Oak, or cedar. Maybe an adze hacked away the bark, maybe a few draw-knife marks, but it's still tree, still round, chunks of its skin left on, bleeding sap, lots of knots—strong enough, though, to hold a man.

Each upright so tall no mother at night might take down a son, no brother a brother. And the cross-strut surely not mortised, fit tight/square to its vertical other, but cruder stuff: hemp-rope to lash the *X* together, coarse fiber, the cross-strut at front, main beam behind, rope laps raising it farther so that a man's deltoids and pectoralis majors are either racked backwards, spine arched out from the upright, or else his arms straight, pinned at wrists and elbows, thoracic vertebrae torqued inward, rolled; he's hunchbacked.

The tying's done on the ground, of course, crowd gathered 'round, a few protesting at first, most goading, quick-tempered, spinning to kick dogs fighting underfoot.

And of the three: do they accede, span themselves over each cross? Not likely.

Struggle, boots to the gut, the men blindsided, bare-knuckled, yanked down, faces struck and kicked, clothes ripped, and their cursing—all three, and all three self-mucused and bloodied and pissed, pinned now at the wrists, ankles crossed and bound, four soldiers to a man, *More rope!* Knives tossed to slice the hemp, and they're stilled now, fixed, the crowd cheering *Yes!*—one of the men in the crowd with a hard-on.

Some few curse the soldiers, their epithets kept under breath.

Three tall crosses, one by one to be raised.

Who dug these goddamn holes? Not deep enough! One-third the length of each pole! Who trained you fools—your mothers?

And the laborers, new men, bend again, fifteen minutes' work, their blades shear rock, much complaint, the tied men still supine, new rubble beside the postholes, and now the call to raise: a soldier at each side of the struts, two at the vertical, they count, lift, the wet wood heavy and the bound man heavy, no balance to be had, pitching backward, swaying, *Lift higher!* says one with a helmet on, and the cross is lifted, lowered into its hole, voice of man on pole dolorous and lost in the crowd, but still it's not plumb, *It's leaning,* and they heave too far left, foolish workmen, compensate now too far right, finally straight, the workmen shamed, angry, *There—now fill it in,* shovelers packing rubble into the hole, slapping it with the back of their blades, the pole-holding soldiers still shouldering it, heroic poses in opposition to each other, more rubble, more soil. *Done. Next one.*

The second one plumbed, and now to the third man, still on the ground, bound, the one they were told to nail. The nails flat-shafted, pounded on an anvil, tapered, black. The man's right wrist bound tight, one nail straight through the capitatum. *That's no pain,* they say, *you woman. Want nails in the tips of your fingers?* Now the left.

The man's feet, wrong in literature and tableau, here crossed at the ankles, bound in hemp, loosed briefly so that each crossed foot can find a surface for nailing. Two men on their knees—each takes a foot, jerks it downward, works it around the side of the post, nails it in. The cord tightened again.

The man himself now, as if oiled: in blood, in sweat, in piss, and the noises he makes animal noises, inhuman. He is raised, the skies leaden, yes, the birds already circling, the soldiers folding their arms, well pleased.

Commentary

Dancers, of course. Sculptors. And many two-dimensional artists—Bruegel, Francesca Woodman, Bacon. Jazz musicians for sure, classical a little less, Bach no, Vivaldi yes, Mahler, Hovhaness … and—my god, Mingus.

All of these arts outside of writing have better access to *body,* to kinetics, than we writers do, and I envy that.

I spend a lot of time in Paris, never tire of museums, even if it's to sit down before a single painting for half an hour, leave.

One year not too long ago I was sitting before yet another crucifixion scene (am an ex-Catholic, yes, but the levels of allegory still stir me), and I must have been in a lousy mood, because I found myself a little pissy over the sterility of the scene depicted. (Could it have been Tournier? I don't remember now.) *Story* was there, certainly, but not much *body.*

We have these bodies. They work, they sweat, they take pleasure, they hurt, they fail. I didn't see any of that there, felt a push.

It's rare that I begin a prose poem with conscious intention to *treat a subject,* even to go from Place A to Place Z. But here, combining my aversion to that sanitized scene with my own history of labor (carpentry, plumbing, endless digging) with an aversion to writers who do a single lick of work in a space of ten years & rush to write a poem about it ("Chopping Pinewood on a Snowy Evening," etc.) I felt compelled to try to get it right—the details of it—to attempt entry into the mad dance of bodies involved in such a scene, sense of propulsion, the drive toward completion pushed along in the poem by the pulse & great wealth of language we're offered, attempt to get a sense of repressed sexuality & the victims' impotence, of voice & viscosity, violence, a final brief silence.

(I think the piece works best when read aloud.)

Carolyn Forché

The Colonel

What you have heard is true. I was in his house. His wife carried a tray of coffee and sugar. His daughter filed her nails, his son went out for the night. There were daily papers, pet dogs, a pistol on the cushion beside him. The moon swung bare on its black cord over the house. On the television was a cop show. It was in English. Broken bottles were embedded in the walls around the house to scoop the kneecaps from a man's legs or cut his hands to lace. On the windows there were gratings like those in liquor stores. We had dinner, rack of lamb, good wine, a gold bell was on the table for calling the maid. The maid brought green mangoes, salt, a type of bread. I was asked how I enjoyed the country. There was a brief commercial in Spanish. His wife took everything away. There was some talk then of how difficult it had become to govern. The parrot said hello on the terrace. The colonel told it to shut up, and pushed himself from the table. My friend said to me with his eyes: say nothing. The colonel returned with a sack used to bring groceries home. He spilled many human ears on the table. They were like dried peach halves. There is no other way to say this. He took one of them in his hands, shook it in our faces, dropped it into a water glass. It came alive there. I am tired of fooling around he said. As for the rights of anyone, tell your people they can go fuck themselves. He swept the ears to the floor with his arm and held the last of his wine in the air. Something for your poetry, no? he said. Some of the ears on the floor caught this scrap of his voice. Some of the ears on the floor were pressed to the ground.

Commentary

I wrote the poem in a single night on an electric typewriter that faced a window tufted with frost. Between the sentences of the poem, I watched the snow fall on the other side of the black glass. The room was painted white and did not belong to me. I was not present in the room during the writing of the poem, but somewhere else. I was there again, in the colonel's house, typing from memory verbatim the details of that night because one day I thought I might write about it and I didn't want to forget anything. I worried that I would forget but I need not have: everything still comes back very precisely and sometimes in slow motion although the night I was taken to talk with the colonel is now forty years in the past. The poem that was not intended to be a poem emerged as a cube, shaped like a room. The moon in the poem hangs from a black cord the way a lightbulb hangs from the ceiling of an interrogation room. It may have to do with a trick of the mind, turning the room into the site of an interrogation. Or that is what I have thought at times in the years since. The parrot said hola not hello. I could have written hola but kept it in English. As children, we used to press our ears to the ground to listen for trains coming. Trains about to arrive. In that sense, we were listening for something that would happen in the time to come. I know that dead ears cannot hear anything. I know that. I had no power to convey the colonel's sentiments to the American president.

Charles Fort

Requiem for the Twenty-First Century (Darvil Meets James Brown in Harlem and New Orleans)

Darvil is locked inside a cage. He feels a stiletto at the back of his neck and into his heart under absolute night and he is asleep on the hollow street and the slow kiss of gin and music begins to boil in his eyes and he ends his day in Harlem in search of New Orleans and his life turns to holy dust the minute a train whistle curdles the ears and he finds himself inside the blue bark rubber tree at the edge of Harlem a forest full of buckwheat and heroin at his feet and his blackened eye hovers above his head above a toilet inside a stool pigeon apartment next door to the sheriff of Paris and he hears the echo of the bright angels who drive a taxi and sell their plasma to the underworld and he becomes the gemstone confidence man and prime mover of Harem real estate who rises in a rotating world beyond the world and the stars, moon, and ocean align with mother mulatto and he blows a kiss to wealth and blood in a five and dime rest home and he awakes in his urine like a stone ass frigate and ice cubes between his legs and he believes he is on fire god and he is not in love tonight as the sailor rope tightens his penis between his puppet legs and he falls backstage in the Apollo Theater and takes a drink of applejack for the pain begins to twist his backbone and rattles the cage in his brain and he finds the crowd in a rage of sex, snow, and remembrance and he sees a man who holds his sex in his charred hands and watches a low target missile silo on a midnight moonshine raid rise three stories between his frosted legs into what he thought was a rubber doll but the electric socket tells its own story and the crowd goes wild and they wipe their foreheads with dish rags and pig ass and he looks out on the fire escape and sees a city chicken begging for sourdough bread until it flies above his head and the limousine driver drives the jazz crowd home for Ovaltine and cookies and a shower and he believes he is at the Cotton Club and feels like a rat in a pill box and he has whooping cough on the subway and hears jazz under the royal pony of the tracks and a man with a jack-o'-lantern and it gives him hope and sufficient sleep to wake and read his poetry under the angelic street like a black tempest in the unforgivable world of color and rage and he finds he is on the street of the black and bronzed god on streets paved in high yellow in front of a rent party and to enter he must place his face against a candle and a paper bag for if he has the wrong color skin color and is too dark and wrong color he is thrown out on the street and rolled into a manhole and he has ten minutes to find a home in a corridor without light and he looks out from the manhole and sees a neon figurine in front of turkey red eyes and tries to carry the bird home and in the morning he finds a two-dollar bill tied to his toe and a pig's foot burning between his legs and he jumps from the fire escape like a black jackal in heat and falls in the snow and turns his eyes and falls back asleep and he knows he has to leave this sharecropper city on both of his legs or he will ignite in heaven and he sees a shoe shine boy who looks like his son lick the monkey feet of the money man for a two cent tip and fish heads and with no good sleep in a just and miniature world he is drowsy and falls on his knees and needs a free market resurrection against the cold fog and Sunday morning three minutes to dawn and the children mothers and fathers enter their church and he cannot warn them about Birmingham for the ropes will be pulled and the bells will be pulled and he covers his face with shaved ice and leaves his bow tie and shark skin suit at the dry cleaners and pulls down a cab and falls out in front of a juke joint and he learns it had burned down last night like angel wings in hell and he feels the subway under his feet and looks down into the sidewalk grate and sees a trail of prairie schooners and slave ships under a christmas tree and tinsel falling from the chariot sky and hand his address changes before his brown eyes and he cannot remember his name, her pretty lace, this place, these people and there is sourdough bread on the linoleum floor an outside his cell a rat shouts on the telephone and the naked guard places a penny in each of his eyes and prays for his soul to heal where it sleeps and his hour is gone and he rides on a buffalo and leaves Harlem on a buffalo on his way to New Orleans and he wears cowboy boots and carries a gold lasso and heads south to the mouth of the Mississippi on the southern crescent and then back around the world and his tale of one long shadow of a man and the story will be like sweet fire a requiem for the twenty-first century. *Please, Please, Please. Don't Go.* James Brown. Harlem. 1962. Apollo Theater. Mississippi Queen. Darvil sits in the front row two hours before show time his elephant ears and alligator eyes drift to a black cajun a drummer like a waterfall bass player in the rocky mountain fat back Americana rent party on a twenty-four-hour street corner rock and roll born and stamped Grade A by the bastard blues and subway hummingbirds feed on race records found sunny side up on a brownstone Victrola and 78s thrown to a black-bottom mama by a big daddy in a nine piece suit woven in the harlem renaissance fire hydrant hot sauce crawfish hand out by a social worker in a farmer's market mango pie in the glove compartment of a three story Cadillac collards in every two-door garage masthead alley cat wrecking crew in grand central station shoe shine polish and Murray's Pomade on the chained ankles of the Pullman Porter-of-Promise on the night train headed to the continent of kings a window cleaner on the fifty-ninth floor and a bucket of catfish in New Orleans. *Try Me.* 1982. Engaged to be wed. Mississippi Queen floats on a red river midnight saxophone and Junior Walker and the All-Stars. *What Does It Take* on a full moon carousel of bourbon and beer baroque barbecue goat ribs alligator pie mardi gras mambo mardi gras mambo street car lizard smokes a Cuban cigar five minutes to show time ain't no potato like blackberry jam.

Commentary

The origins of this poem might one day surpass Darwin's *The Origin of the Species.* I state this because my main character is the prehistoric time-traveler *Darvil,* a three-foot minotaur in patent-leather shoes, large brown eyes, appendages over its entire body, webbed feet, and a six-foot red tongue that snaps like a whip. *Darvil* plays blackjack under the evolutionary light. My prose poem trilogy, *Darvil,* has metamorphosed into a tetralogy. I was under Bloom's Anxiety of Influence and based my prose poem sequence, in part, on *Leo Africanus,* companion to W. B. Yeats, Ellison's *Invisible Man,* Richard Bruce Nugent's, *Smoke, Lilies, and Jade,* and Wright's *The Man Who Lived Underground. Darvil* is The Other— my gentleman-magic-man. As poet-in-residence at Xavier University of Louisiana for three years, I became the first editor and co-founder of *The Xavier Review.* During my time in New Orleans I attended three Mardi Gras, three Jazz Festivals, three of everything. Lucky number. My fiancée and I boarded the *Mississippi Queen* steamboat that left the riverbank for two hours. There were long bars and longer drinks on both levels. Music and Dancing, The first hour on the first level we were entertained by Junior Walker and the All-Stars: *What Does it Take.* On the second level James Brown and the Mighty Flames: *Try Me.* They say Neptune lost his sea legs that evening. I started writing "Requiem for the Twenty-First Century (Darvil Meets James Brown in Harlem and New Orleans)" at the Café Du Monde aided by café au lait and beignets. I became engaged in New Orleans to my late wife Wendy. We fell in love on the *Mississippi Queen.* We wed in Connecticut. Twenty-five years.

Stephen Frech

10.

Blind children stop in the city square to listen to the puppet show, the high-pitched voices the puppeteer lends to the characters, the wood club landing on the hard head of another, the peals of laughter from the crowd, the tale of romance in which true love wins out over deception and lust.

Adults chaperoning the children narrate the action for them, what had they not been blind they could have seen for themselves: the man with a hooked nose enters; he has a silly, pointed hat too small for his head; she is on stage, but he can't see her. Such simple actions.

And for those realizations that defy description, the children will not know but for their own broken hearts: she's crushed; she cannot believe he lied to her; she cannot believe she's left the man who truly loves her.

The adults cannot narrate this action or simply cannot bring themselves to say the words. And for those children who do know, they will lose faith in those adults to guide them, or they will develop a sympathy and take their hand when they leave and never want to let go.

Commentary

This scene appears in *A Palace of Strangers Is No City,* a twenty-two-section sequence of prose poetry that maintains a sustained narrative about two lovers on opposite sides of an occupied city. The puppet show, familiar in its archetypes, mirrors many of the themes in the larger story: dark tones and foreboding, disorientation, desperation, and a love that must fight against its circumstance.

The children, without falling prey to the puppet show's deliberate ruses and disguises, understand with heightened sensitivity the central heartbreak, the dominant theme of betrayal at the heart of the story. The children feel it profoundly in ways their sighted chaperones can't know.

Separated from the larger sequence as it is here, the puppet show reads as a stand-alone prose poem: hybridized, embedded, situated in narrative, but functioning independently of that narrative. Lyric poems, prose or verse, often function in this way—liberated from their narrative context, they carry with them the mood and felt experience of the moment.

Prose can wonder more easily than poetry. Its discursive nature reaches for connection, tends toward sorting through for the sake of making sense. Poetry, in articulating felt experience, gives language to the unsayable, sometimes the unknowable. The tradition of prose poetry hybridizes these narrative, discursive tendencies of prose with the imagistic, elliptical tendencies of poetry.

Prose poetry's resistance to easy definition provides a well-made vessel for the irreal, the surreal, and the themes of knowing in my sequence, the same challenges of knowing inherent in life.

Jeff Friedman

Judges

After the guest ate all the potatoes and the whole brisket, after he ate the tzimmes, the roasted beets and the fruit cocktail, he called for Elijah to enter the door, for Elisha to send a hatchet on the water, for Joshua to blow his trumpet. He called for Moses to drum up more business in this poor economy. He touched his Star of David. He touched the mezuzah on the door. "Something's wrong," he said. "This house has lost its harmony." "What can we do?" we asked. He didn't answer. Instead he ate the chickpeas, the hummus and all the leavened and unleavened bread. He ate the honey cake and the prune pudding. What else could we feed him? Would he fix the piece of Torah nailed to our doorway? Would he bring peace? Would he boil the pots and pans and say a prayer? Would he rock back and forth in his white shawl? Next, he ate the porcelain bowls, plates and all the silverware, then the glasses and tablecloth. He ate the chairs and the dinner table and then the couch and coffee table. He ate our phones so we couldn't call for help. He ate the dust, the particles of debris and shed skin, the shadows with their long threats, the voices rising from the floorboards, the blessings that failed to bless. When he finished, when the place was empty, he looked us over, flashing his teeth. As we backed away from him, he belched loudly, said a prayer. "That should take care of the problem," he announced. Now there was nothing left to fight over, but nothing was more than enough.

Commentary

The title comes from the Jewish Bible. I've always written midrashic pieces (stories and poems that reinterpret biblical texts), and this would fall into that category though I was not retelling or reinterpreting any particular Jewish story. During the course of the story, I alluded to Moses, Elisha, and Elijah. I structured the prose poem around the idea of waiting for Elijah during the Passover seder, leaving a door open for him to enter. The guest invited to dinner is a rabbi, who recognizes that there may be some discord in the household. The rabbi is a composite character based on at least three different men from my youth—one a rabbi, one a poet, and one a prophet (Samuel), all of whom were brilliant, but also pushing the edge of craziness in their demands on everyone around them. The rabbi in my story first consumes all the food set in front of him and then when he finishes that, he begins to eat everything else, table and furniture included. There is a comic dimension in having a guest literally eat the couple out of house and home. The rabbi may be involved in the task of restoring harmony to the couple or he may actually be a destructive force or he may just be someone who worships a good meal and is used to being fed for free. The narrator in the story isn't sure himself. When the whole thing is over, the man and woman are left with each other, reduced to the anger that has become the norm of their relationship. At the time I wrote this, I was considering writing my own book of Judges using characters from my past, but instead I wrote a book of fables, parables, mini tales, comic sketches, dream stories and other prose pieces, titled *Floating Tales.* I hadn't, at first, thought that I was writing prose poems. I just wrote the pieces as they came to me. It was only later that I recognized that I was really writing prose poems, and that the prose poem allowed my voice to speak in many different voices, with different tonalities. For me, the prose poem crossed a bridge that my verse poems wouldn't cross. The prose poem lived and breathed on other side of the river, for better or worse.

Elisabeth Frost

New Story

They won't even say why they changed it. You had grown used to reports of the small achievements of humans: the invention of flow-through tea bags and cream of wheat, how streets burgeoned from cow paths. There were no lethal leisure suits, no poisons in the hollandaise. You've never seen a lemur, you're not even sure how it's spelled, and as if that weren't enough, the lemur in this new story goes berserk. It starts to weep, and it weeps, they say, until its fur prunes and the only sound it makes is of fluids traversing hidden ducts. It feels no hunger, only thirst, and as its nails grow unchecked, it knows that weeping is its job now, that there is no reason for it, or if there is, it's of no importance. The end. Bawling yourself by now, you beg for the sweet story of the electric outlet. You clamor for the one about how the Mallomar got its name, or your favorite of all—the short but vivid history of the mimeograph.

Commentary

When a story becomes familiar, we can hold it in one palm—a well-rubbed talisman. We know its contours in our bodies, while in our minds, it supplies sequence where we are most afraid—primally, viscerally—there is none.

In the country in which I was born, the story was about how much better everything had gotten and will always get. The story was about progress. Dips might mar the curve, but the line of history progressed inevitably upward, asymptotic, toward perfection.

I recently traveled with an artist friend to see the cave paintings at Chauvet. Photos can't capture the scale, nor the complex surfaces—

irregular, sloped, bumpy—on which the artists worked. One image, created by blowing ochre pigment against a hand pressed to the wall, revealed the small appendages of a Paleolithic being 30,000 years ago. The hand resembled a series of deep coves, like the calanques of southern France, with their sharply curving coastlines. It was hard to choose which I loved more, the hand or the bison. These were depicted in profile—haunch, femur, hoof, tail, belly, hump, ear, eye, snout. The bison clamored in a headlong run. We watched them, and we heard from our guide that diminishing size in one quadrant of the drawing denoted distance. Perspective! My artist friend said she might as well give up—how could anyone today match the spare power of these images?

For her, as for me, progress is the most dubious story of them all.

In the square box of the prose poem—the shape I prefer for mine—the self-consciousness of story is always present. The prose poem allows for open, unstrained speculation. It allows for logical leaps, without the formal distractions of lineation or the visual ones of field composition. In this open realm, where image and narrative coexist with ease, I like to ask what the story really is.

When I wrote this piece, I was thinking about what happens when we take for granted a story that suddenly crumbles like sandstone in a tight grip.

The truth is my friend and I didn't see the cave paintings. The paintings are deep underground in a maze of interior rooms. They are preserved there, guarded. What we saw was an elaborate facsimile, a simulacrum, a sort of archaeological mimeograph. Even as we were grateful for access to a meticulously recreated version of the original, even as we were moved by the experience, my friend and I felt taken, too. Like cherishing a memory of Paris only to recall with a jolt that what you'd seen was the Eiffel Tower in Vegas. We weren't sure which version of our own narrative to believe.

Who tells us the stories about culture, about history, that we come to hold in our hands? What do we do when a familiar narrative is blitzed, replaced with something bleak, terrifying?

We may be powerless over the content of stories we are told, but we are never powerless over meaning.

Besides, remembering is what some of us do best.

The tension between sequence and time-defying leaps thrives in the paradoxical "form" of the prose poem.

Perhaps that's what led me to the device at the end of this piece—the mimeograph.

I am old enough to have worked many a mimeograph machine, to recall the acrid smell of its watery ink, to see clearly, with a measure of delight, its purple remains on my fingers.

Richard Garcia

Chickenhead

Chickenhead makes me think of Jesus. Even though Jesus died on the cross for our sins and Chickenhead was just a hood who died hanging from a meat hook. First, take the Romans—Italian, right? In other words, gangsters. Take hanging from a cross and hanging from a meat hook. Both ways, you die slow.

Chickenhead used to shoot the heads off chickens in his backyard when he was a kid. Jesus used to play with birds when he was a kid too. Except, instead of blowing them apart, he would put them together.

Chickenhead was a big shot on the block. In more ways than one, since he weighed three hundred pounds. When Chickenhead got in the back of his Cadillac it would tilt to one side. Jesus was big in his neighborhood too. But he was skinny. When Jesus would get on a donkey—maybe it was an old, decrepit, almost dead donkey—that donkey would trot along skimming over stones as if it had wings.

Jesus made people mad. Chickenhead made people mad. Skimming a little off the top is O.K., it's expected. But after Chickenhead bought that second Cadillac, and after what he did to that Gypsy girl in the back room of the cleaners with her dad forced to watch, he had to go. The Romans had dice. We had dice. The Romans had a wooden cross. We had a meat hook. The Romans had spears and vinegar. We had a bucket of cold water and one of those electric cattle pokers.

Chickenhead hung there. We'd give him a splash and an electric goose once in a while. His whole body would shimmer, all blubbery. Took Jesus three hours. Took Chickenhead three days.

Jesus got famous. First guy to beat Death at his own game. Nobody remembers Chickenhead but me. And if some stranger, a cop maybe, asked, Did I know Chickenhead? I'd play it safe just like Saint Peter when he heard that cock crow—once, twice, three times—and I'd say, I never knew nobody named Chickenhead.

Commentary

There always seems to be some confusion about the prose poem, or at least, different opinions about what it is, what it is not. I have had prose poems published in fiction sections of journals. I have seen versions of my own prose poems posted in blogs, but lineated by editors who apparently think there was a formatting mistake they should correct.

I seem to be clear on what the prose poem is and is not, and am able to explain it. I teach graduate students about it. And yet, it appears I am not always so sure. My poem "Diorama" was first published in *Solstice* as a lineated poem, and later I rewrote it as a paragraph and included it in *Porridge,* a book of prose poems. I like both versions.

My prose poem "Chickenhead" appeared in Peter Johnson's journal *The Prose Poem: An International Journal* under a different title, "Just Like Saint Peter." The same piece is in a chapbook called *Chickenhead* and in my collection entitled *Rancho Notorious.* A blogger in Holland translated it into Dutch for his blog, where it is called "Kippen-Kop." (I kind of like that title.) It appears in the anthology *The Best of the Prose Poem* and the online version of that anthology, webdelsol.com, as "Chickenhead." In some of these versions the first sentence of each paragraph is indented, and in some it is not. I have come to think that it's becoming a convention for full justification to indicate a prose poem, not a paragraph of prose.

So, "Chickenhead" appears in different places, sometimes with different titles or different formatting. It is a dramatic monologue—a person, who is not me, is speaking. He is telling the reader a story about a hoodlum called Chickenhead. As he describes him, he makes a strange comparison between Chickenhead and Jesus. Though he is careful not to implicate himself in the murder of Chickenhead, he does seem to have a lot of information on the specifics of the crime. He may not be the most reliable narrator; something about his way of talking tells us who and what he is, some kind of low-level gangster, definitely a bullshitter, like some lowlife out of a Damon Runyon story.

One of the first things I tell my students about the prose poem is, it does not have characters. The subject is a kind of emblem, or some general voice, like "A Man," "The Woman," or "A Dog," or even an object, but not a named character. In a prose poem, a man goes to the thrift store to buy a used trout stream; John Smith does not. The speaker in "Chickenhead" is anything but generic.

Another thing I tell them is, prose poems are often based on the fable, and generally start with an absurd proposition. "Chickenhead makes me think of Jesus," while not something you hear everyday, hardly qualifies as absurd.

I have come to think that, by my own rules on what is and what is not a prose poem, I'm busted! "Chickenhead" is a piece of short fiction, not a prose poem. At least, for now.

Amy Gerstler

Bitter Angel

You appear in a tinny, nickel-and-dime light. The light of turned milk and gloved insults. It could be a gray light you're bathed in; at any rate, it isn't quite white. It's possible you show up coated in a finite layer of the dust that rubs off moths' wings onto kids' grubby fingers. Or you arrive cloaked in a toothache's smoldering glow. Or you stand wrapped like a maypole in rumpled streamers of light torn from threadbare bed sheets. Your gaze flickers like a silent film. You make me lose track. Which dim, deluded light did I last see you in? The light of extinction, most likely, where there are no more primitive tribesmen that worship clumps of human hair. No more roads that turn into snakes, or ribbons. There's no nightlife or lion's share, none of the black and red roulette wheels of methedrine that would-be seers like me dream of. You alone exist; eyes like locomotives. A terrible succession of images buffets you: human faces pile up in your sight, like heaps of some flunky's smudged, undone paperwork.

Commentary

It's a little difficult to remember what in blazes I was thinking about when I wrote this poem, simply because the year it was written in seems so long ago now, that I almost feel as though I dreamed 1989 rather than lived in it for a while, along with many other beings alive at the time. Stumbling down memory lane, scanning for landmarks, I seem to recall wanting to construct a poem that pondered a besmirched deity—one as imperfect, harried, and untidy as I usually feel myself. I wanted to postulate an "angel" prey to human frailty—not exactly a new idea, but I decided to try to construct my personal version.

There's a train in the poem because I love trains and have a bad habit of trying to insert them into every text I get my hands on. Ditto toothaches and moths. I'm pretty sure the title came from a mishearing. Maybe someone mumbled, "little arrangement" or "little ranger" or "twitter danger" or "bitten bagel" and I heard the phrase which makes up the title instead, and so I began to wonder about ways in which one of God's messengers might be constructed as "bitter."

It would likely be an angel assigned to the bad news delivery division, I thought, a heavenly emissary who might be prone to bitterness temperamentally, and/or whose appearance might signal bitter tidings to those who saw him. A conflicted harbinger of misfortune, full of misgivings, with a crummy job and maybe even bad eyesight.

The early part of the poem is an attempt to play with images of whiteness I liked to use in poems at the time and then subvert, dirty up a little. It was also an attempt to set up a kind of "mood lighting," where the images in the poem are seen via a murky kind of light, not unlike the fading illumination in old, black-and-white movies which are aging poorly and therefore look dimmer and dimmer when projected. Hence the image of a silent film in the middle of the poem. I hoped that this type of uncertain, strain-your-eyes lighting would convey a sense of seediness and unease that was at odds with some conventional ideas of angelhood, virtue, or goodness.

The poem was an attempt to try to fuse the angelic and the tawdry; the holy and the lowlife; the earthly and the celestial. This particular marrying of seemingly opposite elements is an abiding interest of mine for a number of reasons, not the least of which is that such a fusion is central to my sense of what it's like to be human—to be a seething container of the mystic, the quotidian, and the sinister, among other things.

Ray Gonzalez

Seams

Eunuchs spit on temple walls to redefine the origin of water that seeped between their legs to give birth to what Dante dreamed and why Darwin caught a Martian disease, the island of Komodo dragons lifting out of the sea to lay their eggs in his white hair. Even all the hidden passageways want a name in the history books because Galileo died blind and Mozart was addicted to billiards. Their last wishes are hidden inside secret files immune to erasure, their temples overrun with thoughts that marry Ouilipian faith in the bent fork and a Whitman eyelash with the lice removed from Rimbaud's head. The hotel doorman is denied Arthur's manuscripts because Paul Celan translated from eight languages and Emily Dickinson left 1,775 poems behind, a prayer shawl left in the town square where Joan of Arc burned, finding infinity as a marble caught in Andre Breton's throat the night surrealism died.

Commentary

The prose poem is a compressed visionary window where perception is released through the tight spaces formed by sentences that serve the same function as lines and stanzas in linear verse. This is nothing new to poets who use the prose poem as a lightning strike—sharp window, relentless sentences regardless of subject matter or tone, and central images hard to overcome. History in "Seams" is thrust forward to be re-experienced, as far as any prose poem can be comprehended, with a reliance on the sentence as the vibrant form. My choice to rewrite these facts in prose changes the linear vacuum of revelation toward a poetics of fleeing imagery that propels the paragraph forward. Prose poetry is some of the most restless writing we have because trusted sentences develop in a surreal world whose islands overflow with dragons and famous figures tagged in a paragraph that will never stand still. They are not necessarily identifiable characters because my prose evolves through movement of the unexpected and the formerly familiar. Even the narrator of the poem is unknown. Is it the poet researching history to gather strange moments together and hoping it works? Did one of these iconic names step forward from historic mystery to participate in the completion of a dark paragraph—dark as in the block text and dark in the way things happened? The poet is in the text somewhere and his presence means all is true. A prose poem is never fiction. No debate required. The prose poem paragraph stands alone, in its acceleration, more than a costumed linear creation does. Over the years, I have found that readers question the content of my prose poetry less than they do my linear poems. Most readers want everything explained in a traditional stanza because it is open and waiting for the reader to react. Prose poems do not wait because it is the grammatical nature of the vibrant poetic paragraph to consume all barriers as it releases time through catharsis, revolving in a space where no questionable stanza can dwell because a prose poem contains a textual makeover inside literary dimensions unreachable in lines and stanzas. Why? Ask Darwin. When poets say they feel freer writing prose instead of broken lines, they have already tapped the scaly nose of the Komodo and there is one ship still waiting for them in the rocky harbor.

Daniel Grandbois

On First Looking into Campbell's Chunky

A baby's preserved face poked out a porthole to give me the news.

"You're joking," I scoffed.

"If I were, could I do this?" Yet, no action was taken, save the passing of its ship in the night.

What I'd assumed to be guideposts bobbed into buoys that sharpened further into focus as heads above the soup.

"Beautiful day," I addressed the nearest.

"Not from where I sit."

Was this abuse or disabuse, a *Fuck you!* or a favor? In life I would have known.

"Top of the morning to you," I called to another.

"More like bottom of the night."

"Not from where I sit," I countered unconvincingly.

I'd believed I was in some sort of boat but found that my head was bobbing with the rest.

"Could you pass the salt?"

"Which way to Pensacola?"

"Ah, there you are," said a third to no one in particular.

I opened my mouth to respond but said instead, "Goodnight, princess," and pursed my lips as if to kiss my daughter's head.

Her head was not there, of course. As with all those apples still in the orchard, it remained stuck on its tree.

Oh, the orchards! Wave after wave of trunks and limbs! What textures and growths! What colors and scents!

Ah, but all fruit must fall. Or, rather, be plucked by the hand that harvests and then ferries away to that undiscovered country, which, as it turns out, is but a soup.

The question is, whose bowl restrains it, whose spoon comes a-fetching?

Commentary

Is this a prose poem? Experts in every field disagree on the interpretation of data. MacArthur Fellow Lydia Davis interprets Russell Edson's work as stories. My pieces have been published as stories, poems, flash fiction, prose poems and PP/FF (Peter Conners' clever term). Yet, the work is all of one blood, and I wrote this way before I knew half of those terms existed.

There was a period, however, when I wrote the way I thought one should write. It felt like beating my head against a wall. After a workshop in Iowa, I pestered the clerk at Prairie Lights for books as unbounded as Brautigan's. He handed me *The Tunnel* by Russell Edson. I stopped trying to write like Carver and Hemingway and returned to my natural voice. I'd already written a novel in it, which I now recognized as a series of linked prose poems (though it was eventually published with illustrations as an art novel and subtitled *An Hallucinated Memoir*).

Write what you write, and let the chips fall where they may.

Cathryn Hankla

What Falls

In the morning, I could already hear my downspouts clattering like bumbling skunks, the likes of which had been a midnight plague up until the rains came chasing Pepé's cousins under the half- finished porch next door. One night I'd heard a certain thump followed by a screech or merely a fierce squeak, and then a pungent waft slammed me back onto my pillows. Oh boy, it was bad, and set me to wondering how long its plume would last, how enveloping it might become, when the fumes subsided or crested their wave, at least growing no worse, and the realization crashed over me that perhaps the skunk had sprayed next door, and what I'd just been treated to was a shifting of the winds. Not so with freezing rain, however, which fell everywhere at once. Barking dogs could not chase it away. Nothing would end about this weather for me, until everyone in town was no longer dripping wet if not exactly dry again.

Commentary

This started as a six-minute free-write I did with one of my classes. It was raining that evening, so we took the path of least resistance as our prompt. Good enough for Guillaume Apollinaire, I thought. There has been so much stink around us, and neighbor set upon neighbor in the smallest and broadest sense of the word. The folksy tone embodies what it means to be placed in a community, the long and short sentences meant to capture a story-telling rhythm that might be hampered if this were arranged into lines. The rain falls on everyone, a truism (and biblical, Matthew 5:45), and a good reminder that our individual situations are inextricably linked to collective experience.

Marie Harris

LOUIS ANTOINE DE BOUGAINVILLE, WHO CIRCUMNAVIGATED THE GLOBE (1766-1769), ENCOUNTERING NOBLE SAVAGES, CANNIBALS, ADVENTURE, STARVATION, ETC., IN HIS QUEST FOR UNKNOWN ISLES AND CONTINENTS, DISCOVERS LONGBOAT KEY IN THE OFF-SEASON.

—23 May

We anchor in a bay and put ashore in several boats, approaching the settlement by one of the many man-made canals. Red-throated, long-beaked birds hang on the trunks of banyan trees. All manner of shore birds fly and fish in the shallows; some of our number are well-occupied recording their shapes and cries while others busy themselves at the listing of flowers which run from yellows to deep purples and seem to have been cultivated for some purpose we cannot readily discern. Grasses of blue-green hue have been cropped around shallow sandy pits in what appear to be large gaming fields. At intervals, thin sprays of fresh water erupt unbidden from the ground. Enormous white houses of phantasmagorical design, each with a long blue pool shimmering under a delicate opaque structure, occupy every meter of dry land from the verges of the canals to the wide avenues to the raked beaches. We could glimpse no human activity within. There is evidence that the entire population left hurriedly. What rumor? What disastrous news? They must have gone overland. How else to explain the powerful boats abandoned at docks?

Commentary

Sometime in the 1980s I came across a call for submissions of 100 words from a new little magazine (literally, little, as it measured about 3 x 3 inches) called *Paragraph.* I had just finished a draft of a free-verse poem that was vexing me for reasons I couldn't pin down, and I decided to recast it as a prose poem, a form I had first discovered in translations of French poets Charles Baudelaire, Francis Ponge, and Jean Follain and in the work of American poets as diverse as Walt Whitman, Gertrude Stein and Russell Edson. I had even written a few collected under the title "Wives" in my first book but had not pursued it further until I undertook this exercise. It was unexpectedly satisfying. "Weasel in the Turkey Pen" was accepted and became the title poem of my second book.

I began to write more poems in the form, hardly aware of the reason for its appeal. Only as I reread my output over the following months did it occur to me that it was its narrative possibilities that had drawn me. I could tell my short, dense stories without abandoning any of the devices of poetry save the line break. Even rhyme remained available, albeit in subtle ways. I continued to experiment, insinuating more and more elements into the form's rather elastic container. I incorporated fragments of letters and journal entries, bits of instruction manuals, snatches of overheard conversations. It became the ideal (perhaps the only) way I finally found to tell the story of the wounded 14-year-old boy we adopted into our family.

But perhaps the most unanticipated surprise of the form was its capacity to embrace humor. Not the humor of light verse, with its wit and wordplay, but a more nuanced, almost deadpan approach to our shared peculiarities. I began to explore and enjoy the possibilities of allowing another element, another layer into my poem narratives.

I love to laugh. Louis Antoine's "logbook entry" makes me laugh.

Bob Heman

Perfect

She was perfect. There was no other way she could be. When the serpent came to her he taught her how to look at her own image in the surface of the water. He gave her paints to color her lips and eyes and a scale so she could see how much she weighed. "You are not pretty enough," said the serpent. "You are not thin enough. He will not want you." She heard every word he said and began her descent from perfection.

Commentary

This simple little piece is actually part of a much larger series of over 350 very small prose poems that bounce off of the legends of the Serpent and the Garden, frequently in irreverent or unexpected ways.

My first exposure to the story of the Garden of Eden was as a child, when I attended Lutheran Sunday school every week at the church where my parents were members. As I grew older and started reading science fiction and fantasy, and later writing stories of my own, I became fascinated by tales of the beginnings of things—of how the universe, and life, and even our own consciousness began. For me the legends of the Garden became the story of the origin of human consciousness, of the evolution of our own self-awareness.

In early April 2000, I started writing some short prose poems that were inspired by the tales of the Garden. Excited by these new pieces, I decided that I would write nothing else during that month, and did just that, and then continued my resolve through the month of May and into the first days of June, during which time I wrote almost nothing else. I had become totally locked into the process and ended up with 235 small poems inspired by the stories of the Serpent and the Garden.

A few years earlier, when I started writing primarily in pocket notebooks (mostly on the train), I had begun a series of very small prose poems, frequently no larger than three to five lines, which were to become the beginnings of my ongoing "information" series. The new pieces I started that April were essentially a continuation of that series but soon took on a life of their own as a separate group. At first, I called the new pieces "The Garden Variations," but after returning again to the series in 2005 and adding another 107 poems, I started calling them "The Serpent Variations." I have continued writing them occasionally ever since, although never in the same focused way, and now frequently refer to them simply as "The Serpents" or "The Serpent Poems." Usually, the separate pieces were inhabited by the serpent and the woman and the "other," who, reflecting the woman's perception of him, was never referred to as "the man."

When I first started writing the poems, I was employed in the archives of historic Trinity Church in New York City with the title of Parish Recorder. While the pieces I wrote during that time were not consciously influenced by my working there, I suspect that being surrounded every day by the church and its history may have made me more receptive to what I found myself writing.

Except for when they are presented individually (outside of the context of the series), the serpent poems have never been given separate titles. Instead they have been identified separately only by capitalizing the initial phrase or sentence, in that way emphasizing the series as a whole rather than as individual pieces.

"Perfect" was written on October 19, 2005.

Holly Iglesias

Perishables

In the final days of the war, a boy eats cake, a cake from the saddest mother, a woman unaware that her own son has bled into history, a history with jaws that are soft and tropical, the greenest green, not gray like Lake Erie in winter.

The cake sealed first in waxed paper, then gift wrap, then a grocery bag dismantled with pinking shears, the bundle tied with cotton string, her fingers recalling the tiny buttons of his school shirts, the comb dipped in water before parting his hair.

Mercy rains at every latitude, at each contested parallel, rains anywhere that grunts line up for salt pills, clean socks, for unclaimed parcels that go to those who never get mail.

Cake sweetens the mouth of a boy the woman will never meet, a boy who tastes in the kindness of strangers the complications of survival, a boy who in manhood will crumble each time he tells the tale.

Commentary

C. D. Wright, Rosmarie Waldrop, Susan Howe, Marie Harris, Amy Gerstler, Maxine Chernoff, Nin Andrews, Mary Koncel: these women made me want to write prose poems and they made me want to write about women writing prose poems even when writing prose poems looked like a straight path to obscurity.

So did Gaston Bachelard's *The Poetics of Space,* read aloud in a stagy French accent my first winter alone after a long marriage ended, when I wanted to hide in that cupboard beneath his childhood staircase, to smell the sheets that had been dried in fragrant French air and stored in an armoire with sprigs of rosemary, to peek into cook's pantry in search of candied ginger, to touch anything with a door, a clasp, a pocket, drawers, shelves, compartments.

For me, the great magnet is history, which is sweeping, but I'm compelled to tell it through the material detail, which is fleeting and small and thus poignant. My desire is to tell the big story through the little story—manifest destiny in a pack of darning needles, for example, or immigration through a skate key. My first book, *Souvenirs of a Shrunken World,* helped me recognize this proclivity. The poems take place at the 1904 World's Fair, the largest ever held, an overwhelming encounter with wonder and dread. Visitors were often felled by the experience as well as by the telling of it, thus requiring that it be revealed in small doses, for which a small souvenir served so well—postcards, snapshots, trinkets, all such items functioning as prose poems do, providing pocket-sized intimations of something unbearably large.

In "Perishables," the cake tells the story, or rather a nest of stories—of one woman's loss, one young man's isolation, and of the tragic war that turned the U.S. inside out. It was prompted by hearing a man on the radio relate his experience of getting a package intended for someone else as a young soldier in Vietnam. In the middle of telling the tale, he could no longer speak, sorrow choking back his words. The program's producers did not cut to another feature, but instead allowed a heart-wrenching minute to pass in silence in testament to this enduring grief.

Louis Jenkins

Basketball

A huge summer afternoon with no sign of rain.... Elm trees in the farmyard bend and creak in the wind. The leaves are dry and gray. In the driveway a boy shoots a basketball at a goal above the garage door. Wind makes shooting difficult and time after time he chases the loose ball. He shoots, rebounds, turns, and shoots ... on into the afternoon. In the silence between the gusts of wind the only sounds are the thump of the ball on the ground and the rattle of the bare steel rim of the goal. The gate bangs in the wind, the dog in the yard yawns, stretches and goes back to sleep. A film of dust covers the water in the trough. Great clouds of dust rise from open fields that stretch a thousand miles beyond the horizon.

Commentary

I began writing "Basketball" many years ago when I was in college, but none of the many versions I wrote was satisfactory. Still, it seemed to me that there was a poem in this scene of a boy shooting baskets in a farmyard, so I held on to the image. In the early 1970s, after reading a lot of wonderful work by Robert Bly, Russell Edson, David Ignatow and others, and many translations, I began writing prose poems. Among the first prose poems I wrote was a version of "Basketball."

I found prose to be more malleable than verse, and it allowed for more subtle manipulation of tone and mood. I believed then (and I still believe) that the essence of poetry does not lie in the form of the poem, in the rhyme or meter or beauty of language, or even in meaning, as it is commonly understood. It is rather in the mysterious moment of understanding and empathy one has when reading a good poem, the sudden, almost visceral recognition of a certain truth. I wanted to use language that was clear and unobtrusive, language that allowed the reader the experience without insisting on its "poetic" quality. The prose poem seemed to me to be the right form for my part of the twentieth century.

The prose version of "Basketball" had the effect I wanted: the openness, the flatness, the lack of pretense in language that was right for the scene. Looking at the poem now, I think there is still a bit too much melodrama. The last sentence especially seems overdone, but I wanted to emphasize the extreme feelings of emptiness and endlessness one often has on the Great Plains.

Brian Johnson

Scenes Of Devastation

A poster survived the thunderstorm, but many trees did not. Today I ask myself why the sun fades carpets but ignores flowers. These events look strangely impersonal. While heat makes the entire landscape quiver, water fails to scrub the color out of soap. You love my letters, but I am something else entirely—a heap, a closed fracture, a crumpled box. You can't imagine what losses I try to hide. Yet we deserve one another, even in our disorder. The country of ruins moves us, while the well-preserved village leaves us cold. Nature is the first one to trespass, and every joy or shock follows from that break. It is not only the severed ear in the field—rain dropping from a blue sky—the wild turkeys running up the highway—, it is also the lack of abstinence in our daily weather. The sun is constantly broken, and the wind interrupts our thoughts as if they were a fine error, a pleasing lie. How can we be pure in this climate? When will we stop murmuring and changing our clothes? I am not prepared for a single outing, much less days and days of happiness. When I write to you, I have in mind a country not even the birds will touch, a spot detached from all climates, a place that is neither undiscovered nor deserted, nor idyllic, nor devastated—a real place. I have nothing to show you now, but I have inklings of it. When vegetables grow to enormous sizes, they become tough, inedible. When children grow up, they lose much of their tenderness. With ideas, it is not so. They come out of captivity like giants, and climb over bodies on their way. In time bushes emerge from bald earth, capillaries from rock, and balloons from craters. Yet every transformation is unnatural. Whether the horizon becomes a mall, or a meeting of two stick figures, it disturbs us. My heart wants the old playgrounds and the old looks, but they're made of chalk. Childhood is made of chalk. It exists to the same degree a farm exists in the mirrors of a high-rise, or a family in the crooked drawing: dog, house, sun, flowers, car. I pull out the drawing and return home, thinking that somewhere amidst all the familiar things will be a forgotten note, a glowing relic, the key to this visit and to all the visits preceding it and to the time before visits, when I was the resident child.

Commentary

An ear for cliché—or was it an eye, a nose? I can't remember, but Russell Edson observed that cliché was good for the writing of prose poems. "Scene of devastation" is one such cliché. It comes up whenever we see the remains—of a genocide, a school shooting, a fire, a mudslide. These daily occurrences are not "poetic," if by that we mean "beautiful," but they are overwhelming, they befall us, they bring us to woe.

Woe is the proper subject of the prose poem. Me-woe. World-woe. All those unaccountable things we encounter and might file away with a cliché, but instead return to in something like a poem, half prose, attempting to encompass the loss. As the poem asserts, it is all "strangely impersonal," like wandering through a landscape, being assailed by it, being cut down to size: Macbeth on the blasted heath, or Antonioni's figurines in *L'Avventura,* roving the deserted island.

When I take a walk, I'm overwhelmed by the scale of nature. When I watch the news, I'm overwhelmed by the scale of tragedy. There is no "natural news," as there is no "natural nature." I allude to the severed ear in *Blue Velvet,* which stands for the potential breakdown in any scene, the woe-filled moment, the need to understand what's happening. And whether I write about inner or outer weather; whether the prose poem is realistic, surrealistic, lyric or comic, seems beside the point. We exist in a time when all the weather is not abstinent, all the news is not restrained, all the environments are not right, and yet there is still the need to get settled.

Writing, for me, is the one place where that settlement occurs. I enter it and try to correct places as they are, people as they are, knowing how much misery remains in both. All these digital files fail to eliminate the memory of chalk, my world history wiped from the blackboard and my lucky numbers wiped from the cement.

Peter Johnson

The Millennium

In the basement, in the playroom, Ken's throwing darts at another Ken while the flies of fairy tales nod off on a concrete wall, on a red plunger by the sink, on a lonesome cue ball. Upstairs, a pair of twins dancing on a hardwood floor, pushing tiny Santas in miniature baby strollers. I need help to sit down. "Next you'll be wanting a back rub," my brother says, then leaps from a coffee table, toppling our Christmas tree. Not enough bulbs to poke holes through this night's black logic. No one strong enough to turn The Great Telescope, still partially unwrapped.

Four hours to midnight, my niece embracing her Sleepy-Time Barbie, eyelids set to close at the turn of the century.

Commentary

"The Millennium" is the last poem in *Pretty Happy!*, my first volume of prose poetry. The poem came as a surprise, and it changed everything for me. I'm very fond of *Pretty Happy!*, but, looking back, I see how haunted it was by other texts. I'm thinking of Kafka's parables; Novalis's short prose; the character sketches of the ancient Greek writer Theophrastus (whom I had translated in graduate school); and even things as silly as the "Fractured Fairy Tales" episodes from the *Rocky and Bullwinkle Show* and sketches from my beloved old copies of *Mad* magazine. Those influences were present long before I came to the oneiric landscapes of Charles Simic, Russell Edson, and Max Jacob. That's not to say I didn't have a voice or subject matter. By birth and inclination I'm a mix of high and low cultures. I grew up in a working-class neighborhood near the steel plants in Buffalo, New York, but I went to a Jesuit high school where I studied and translated Greek and Roman classics. It's not surprising that in one of my later prose poems I have Socrates picking a booger from his nose while pontificating on father/son relationships. But how to the find the right way to express my high/low sensibility? How to find a style that was, well, "natural?" I didn't want to write paragraphs that were as mind-numbing as cooking recipes. I didn't want to write prose that was prosaic and that didn't reflect the fragmented way I process the world.

And then "The Millennium" arrived.

It was 1995 and I was back in Buffalo, sledding with my son on Christmas Eve as the world inched its way toward the Millennium. We were riding a sled made from plastic as thin and durable as cellophane. We went hurtling over a snowboarding hump, and when we landed I heard a crack and felt a sharp pain in my back. A half an hour later I was in an emergency room with a number of drunks who had tumbled down the stairs at a Buffalo Bills football game. Three hours later, I was hauled off to Mercy Hospital. I needed no operation but was told if I fell down over the next month or two I probably would be paralyzed. So sitting on a couch in my mother's living room, stoned on Darvocet and Valium, I took in my surroundings, grabbed my notebook, and decided to write a poem. Many of the images and sounds were before or below me: my niece's Barbie and Ken dolls, my mother's artificial Christmas tree, the red plunger by the sink, a lonesome cue ball banging into another ball in the basement.

But then the "flies of fairy tales" appeared, and the poem became a bit more apocalyptic and improvisational, as images and dialogue, real and imagined, collided, with the soundtrack of the Smashing Pumpkins' "Bullet with Butterfly Wings" providing background music from my portable CD player.

For once I never intruded on these images or sounds. Of course the poem went through revisions, but the method, if that is an accurate word for letting one's imagination roam and make unusual leaps and connections, was new and exciting for me. After "The Millennium" I felt comfortable with the poetic process, and most of the poems preceding it in the book were written after it. I no longer was writing with Kafka and my other influences looking over my shoulder. I guess I'm saying that no method was imposed from the outside, or even sought after. The method was me; it was how I thought. It would never assure me of writing a good poem, but at least I'd be writing authentic ones from now on. I would no longer be a copycat. An imposter.

And did the freedom of the prose poem allow me to make this leap? Of course. If I'm walking down the street on the way to a friend's house, I have to stop at traffic lights or make turns. Isn't that what verse poetry is? Isn't that why it's called verse, from the Latin *verto,* to turn. In contrast, the prose poem is like an open pasture where no direction is necessary. Where anything can happen. Where contradictions and juxtapositions (those odd leaps that often transcend logic) are not only welcome but expected—contradictions and juxtapositions that would become even wilder in my next few darkly comic collections.

Alice Jones

Reply

Dear one, remember our moon-set walk across the trestle bridge, trees full of parasitic mistletoe? Are you still eating beef tendon and gristle soup with noodles? My unattended yard now blooms with purple thistles. They fired guided missiles from the mainland, pointed like flying fish, landing with a piscatory splash off-shore. Piss-poor shots, I'd say. The pistil is to stamen as mortar is to pestle, as heart is to well-aimed pistol, as I am to your epistle.

Missing you, yours.

Commentary

The epistolary form felt apt, given the prose poem's block of text is just the right size to fit on the back of a postcard. And after Emily Dickinson's "Letter to the world," isn't every poem a letter from writer to reader? This poem takes that imaginary reach across a gap and makes the letter real.

What initiated this poem, and many in *Gorgeous Mourning,* the book of prose poems from which it is taken, is one sound. I was drawn to the complex friction of the consonants in "istle." From there, I wondered what other letter combinations could produce similar or echoing sounds, hence the various fricatives and "s" sounds throughout. Inside the word "thistle" is the silent second "t," and the voiceless diagraph of the initial "th." This one word embodies a mixture of presence and absence, the colliding consonants, and the unvoiced sounds. When the micro elements of the sounds echo the macro level intentions, this creates another form of rhyme. In the writing, this is not a purposeful arrangement, but the unconscious does the work of linking sound and desire.

The poem as a whole, a love letter, addresses the absent other, who is very present in mind, so present, his frame of reference seems to have taken over the writer's. There are also notes of encroachment, the parasites and weeds taking over, military incursions from mainland China across the Taiwan Strait. Gristle soup happens to be one of my husband's favorite dishes. He grew up in Hong Kong and Taiwan, so the danger of Mao's invasion was a real threat. I think the poem embodies his fear, as well as the love of eating, and then resolves itself with multiple images of penetration. I learned later that the Old English word for thistle was *pistel.*

The four ending forms of entering begin with the flower, its sexual arrangement, move to the man-made mortar and pestle, bowl and phallus, then to the very embodied heart and the very violent pistol, and end in abstraction, the way a letter enters its recipient. Since the original letter to which this is a reply is imaginary, presence and absence are again at play. And spontaneous play is the major mode of the images and sonics in this poem.

George Kalamaras

A Father Kisses His Daughter Goodbye

Based on a photograph in which President Johnson kisses his younger daughter, Luci Nugent, goodbye, as he boards a plane in Austin, Texas, to fly back to Washington—Luci has her two dogs, Kim, a beagle, and a small white stray dog she and her husband adopted, December 10, 1966.

She's young and pretty, and Daddy, boarding the plane, has lips of steel. Not steel, really, as they're softer, flocculent, preparing him to speak the flat grass of Austin back in Washington. His lips are more like water. Sad water. Let's call them blood. Daddy's lips of blood. It's not fair for a man to have to decide who lives and dies. His little girl is a grown woman, still wearing almost-white. A white coat is what we see in hospitals. Where the living come to lie. For a while. Sometimes longer. Hers is an overcoat, gray, in the black and white wash of the past, covering something she doesn't want to be seen. I like Johnson. I detest the man. Not the man, really, but his owl papers and issues of death-flight. Let's call them, *midnight hunt in the Shenandoah Valley for something we can't quite see.* Let's call them, *torn from the belly of a possum.* The mother is crying for her empty pouch. I know it's war in the shagbark of every hickory, in the bones the raccoon collapses to squeeze through the gate. I fear him and his large fatherly kiss. The part in his hair separating wrong from right. The part of his hair that is falling out, like the weeping all over again for those lying useless in the useless jungles across the much-used South China Sea. His hat is large, cocked, trying to keep the lid on things. His wife, dressed in white, is smiling, as all wives in 1966 do or did or refused. *Public* is only one letter more than *pubic,* and what they share in private is likely Johnson peering into the mirror before bed, counting the lost hairs on his scalp. Every follicle of death follows the man. As he boards the plane. As he wanders into the toilet. As he makes water.

Muzzles himself each night before the sheets. *Best not to breed more babies,* he thinks. *We are all born to die.* Sad. Like the Monongahela joining the Allegheny to the Ohio. Which is why the two dogs in this photo are a beagle-hound and a stray. *Daddy loves beagles,* Luci thinks. *So I'll bring him mine to say goodbye.* The stray, all that has gone wrong between them. Between father and watershed. Between rain and the burgeoning banks. Between Daddy and his little river of a now-grown girl. Ever since. Ever since the war got out of control. Crawled out the pouch and shivered, for all to see, on the loose branch of a tree. And all the loss keeps washing up upon the shores. His wife, still in white, watching her husband and daughter embrace, has this happy-sad of a smile. As if she knows the marriage-bed minutes before the mirror that her daughter will not speak. As if she knows the beagle means her husband is still on the scent. Still troubles the black grass with a howl. As if she knows the animal in the stray is lost, then comes to the tarmac some December to almost say, *I once was lost but now am found. Safe travels, Mr. President. Mr. Owl-Flight. Mr. Raccoon-Bones-Collapsed-Before-the-Mirror. Mr. Amazing Ache. Safe travels. Goodbye.*

Commentary

The prose poem, as Robert Bly described decades ago, allows an acceleration of associative leaping. In working in this form off and on since the early 1980s, I have experienced this as well. The form's long lines work similarly on one's consciousness as the elongated breath does, say, during meditation. Hindu yogis long ago discovered the link between breathing and consciousness. As the breath slows, consciousness opens and expands, the psyche becoming increasingly permeable. My experience with the prose poem parallels my experience with meditation. The elongated breath of the line can open gateways into consciousness; the ego's drive to control the poem begins to loosen, allowing the poem to find its focus. This is not to say that one abdicates responsibility for the prose or verse poem's direction. However, similarly to Richard Hugo in his opening chapter in *The Triggering Town,* "Writing Off the Subject," I believe poets need to be courageous enough to relinquish their original intent when writing a poem. For me, this means rethinking the life-force of the poem itself, allowing it to find *itself* in a reciprocal dance between the poet's intent and what the poem itself wants to be.

Yes, *what the poem wants to be.* I have long felt that the poem is alive, that in its wisdom it knows more than the poet. It is essential (even a *sacred* responsibility) to allow the poem to discover what it wants to be. The poet needs to be wise enough *to interact on equal terms* with the poem, allowing the true poem to come unto the tongue. The prose poem can help enable this, often neutralizing opposites, since the form itself questions a series of debilitating binaries, not the least of which are those between poetry and prose as well as poet and poem.

"A Father Kisses His Daughter Goodbye" called to me to be a prose poem from its first stirrings, perhaps because for decades I have felt a rather monolithic critique of President Lyndon Johnson—largely because of his escalation of the Vietnam War. Yet I have had a complicated response, also admiring aspects of his Great Society and progress with Civil Rights.

As a lover of hound dogs—beagles, bluetick hounds, redbone hounds, and others—I have been working on a series of poems and prose poems in which hounds figure prominently, a number of pieces based on old photographs I have collected over the years. Interestingly, several photos are of Johnson and his beagles. I am not just referring to the infamous one in which he picks up one of his beagles by its ears. There are others, tender portraits, including Johnson at his ranch lovingly lounging with his hounds, or a striking photo of his beagles on his lap on Air Force One. This array began to give me a wider lens through which to view the man—a more complex perspective, perhaps due to the animals as conduit. I began to feel compassion for him, though having lost a cousin in Vietnam and having had two others serve there, I have certainly not progressed to the point of being an apologist for Johnson. Just as I have gained a more rounded view, some of the edges that bother me have simultaneously and paradoxically become even sharper.

Donald Hall discusses the necessity of human ambivalence in a poem. It seems to me that the prose poem is particularly well suited for engaging competing feelings, largely because it forgoes a condensing of language in favor of associative leaps, thus encouraging bold—often paradoxical—explorations of the unconscious. Some intertwining realms that "A Father Kisses His Daughter Goodbye" examines are those of public and private, sexuality and war, procreation and power, male and female, and our human and animal selves. How does the human body reveal (betray?) what lies within the unconscious? Think of something as simple as the part in one's hair, suggesting two opposing directions. In completing this poem, I felt more in tune with my long-held critique of Johnson, yet increasingly interested in him as a person—flawed in all his humanness—and not as just an emblem of war madness through which I'd seen him for decades.

Christopher Kennedy

Some Other Species of Love

I walk the perimeter of my living room like the expectant father of a deformed child. I want to wrap myself in yellow crime scene tape and imitate an unsolved murder. I've developed sympathy for antipathy, the thought of gun ownership. My blood desires cool, damp air. My eyes seek to trade places with two black holes, to become a different kind of receptor.

When I look out the window, I see a semi's headlights threaded through the trees. Clouds hang as limp as beached jellyfish. The stars have burned themselves out. The luminous moon is strangely reminiscent. My soul is a memory locked tight in a black box at the bottom of the sea.

I would very much like to find myself among those stars, distant, dead, and gaze upon the planets of some other species of love. But tonight, a monster flexes up from inside me. It wears me like a cocoon. Ladies and gentlemen, the dormant period is over. It has wings. And twenty-four hours to live.

Commentary

Russell Edson's prose poems are the ones that made me want to try to write my own. I resisted the urge, mainly because it seemed silly to imitate a writer whose work was so original, and what could one do except write pale imitations that would be obviously derivative? Then I read somewhere that Edson liked the work of Daniil Kharms, the Russian Absurdist. I read some Kharms, saw the influence on Edson, and began to think in terms of writing prose poems in a tradition rather than in imitation of one particular prose poet. I was familiar with Rimbaud and the French Surrealists from my obligatory Symbolist/Surrealist period, before I seriously considered writing poems myself. Some years later, I heard Charles Simic read from *The World Doesn't End,* which had just won the Pulitzer Prize. I didn't realize he was reading prose poems until I picked up a copy of the book afterwards. Then I read Zbigniew Herbert's prose poems and fell in love with them. I was familiar with James Wright, Robert Bly, James Tate and knew their prose poems as well. It began to seem reasonable to see if I could write some of my own. I wrote prose poems and revised verse into prose poems. I put prose poems into verse and back again, editing for rhythm and pace, cutting what seemed extraneous, adding what was missing and seemed essential.

The early prose poems were fantastical/absurdist/magical realist. I felt freed from the tyranny of the autobiographical poems I'd been writing, and, more importantly freed from the tyranny of the line, a unit of measure I'd become somewhat obsessed with, often to the detriment of other aspects of my work. I wrote with a sense of metaphor that came from the influence of the poets I'd been reading, and I began to trust that what came out would make sense eventually. As I discovered, these prose poems, once I deciphered their meanings and revised them to make as much sense as possible to a reader, were decidedly autobiographical in a different way than my more realistic attempts at free verse. What may have seemed opaque in early drafts became poems about family and friends or political and social realities. Eventually I was able to write with more awareness of my subject while maintaining the same sensibility I developed in those earlier attempts. Those prose poems became a manuscript and eventually evolved into my first book, *Nietzsche's Horse.* In all those early prose poems, narrative was the delivery system for my lyrical impulses.

In "Some Other Species of Love," a poem from my latest collection, *Clues from the Animal Kingdom,* I wrote about suicidal ideation and the rejection of it, conflating the lifespan of a butterfly with the AA slogan "One Day at a Time." In this case, instead of a butterfly emerging from a cocoon, I substituted a monster with wings, the human body an analog for cocoon. To me, the monster is ego, the part of us that always wants to survive, even when some bad mixture of chemicals within us would prefer it be time for lights out. Conflation of the butterfly's lifespan with the rhetoric of the twelve-step philosophy subverts both notions. The twenty-four hours becomes somewhat ominous, the ephemeral, so well-documented by the Romantics, becomes part of the speaker's defense against the appeal of the infinite. Ego defeats the notion of the transcendent, spiritual, hoped for but unknowable afterlife. It's a happy ending after all, one that must be lived out daily.

Christine Boyka Kluge

Where Babies Come From

The door to the hall closet twitched on its squeaky hinges and jangled its brass knob. There were no voices inside, just a rustling, followed by an occasional light thump. The two people in the closet were lost. One of them looked like she was made of rice paper, like fog dried and ironed, then cut in the shape of a woman. She was a translucent ripple moving through the dark, her eyes torn holes, her fingers cottony threads groping in mildewy shadows. Chiming empty hangers, she rummaged in the pockets of winter coats for mothballs and crumpled receipts, old pennies and lint-covered peppermints, then put them to her tissuey lips to suck, as if she could taste her old life again. But each treasure fell through the tear where a mouth would have been, landing on the wood floor with a *plink* or a *crik.*

The other person was an infant girl. She was just arriving to take the woman's place. She kept her eyes closed tight as raisins, but her nose was alert to the scent of wool and cedar and felt boot liners. Due to her rough journey, the top of her velvety head throbbed and her tender spine ached a bit. The closet felt huge and drafty after the last tight room. She twisted her head left and right, burrowing deeper in a cardboard box of unsorted baby pictures. Her umbilical cord draped over the rim like an extension line ready to be plugged in.

As she fluttered from wall to wall, the woman kept tripping on the cord. Perplexed, she searched for a way out, dropping shreds of her flesh like confetti or snowflakes. Her frustrated pacing stirred the air in the closet into a stale, powdery breeze. The baby was cold. Her tongue arched, and her waxy little fists curled into red snails.

When the alarmed couple followed that first warbling cry and opened the closet door, they found a newborn coated with dust, like a chicken dipped in flour, or a baby excavated in Pompeii. They looked down into the startling red cave of her open mouth and saw, not a uvula, but a tiny figure wriggling in her throat—like a paper doll drowning in a well, too stubborn to go down, holding up her white arms in the impossible hope of being lifted.

Commentary

This piece started decades ago, in a coat closet in the entryway of the brick house where I grew up. I can still hear the sound of the closet door opening. I can still smell the mothballs and wool, and picture my father's tweed overcoat dozing on a wooden hanger, coins dated from now-ancient history asleep in its pockets. In the back of the closet, cardboard boxes of unsorted family photographs waited fruitlessly for organization. Even then, some of the older generations in black and white were already curling their scalloped edges. Our baby pictures, class photos and Maine vacation snapshots were shuffled together, swirling time.

This is where the prose poem begins. Its own squeaky door opens to a real space, perfumed with the scent of humans no longer with us. Then it opens wider to encompass an imaginary, mythical place. The closet walls expand to include a ghostly, dying woman and a newborn. Generations, constantly being replaced, unspool over time. Overwhelming. Dizzying. This could be a creation myth.

The rectangular prose poem can become a secret trapdoor that reveals the whispering shadows of the subconscious. In my mind, prose poems are often invitations down into that wilderness, to those unfettered possibilities. When I first read prose poetry, I was attracted to that breadth of dreamy imagination, to that freedom and ease with which writers accessed deeper, darker places. I felt welcomed to the widest and wildest writing.

Are prose poems funnier than regular poems? In my writing I think they are. This may have something to do with that perceived permission to unleash the imagination. Poetry and humor already have much in common. They both take disparate ideas and join them in a surprise of beauty/shock/laughter. But the prose poem delights in what I call the twisted little laugh. For instance, in this piece, it is so sad that the woman is dying, that she is not ready to depart. We can't help her! It's too late. But that horrific moment of being swallowed and replaced by the squalling newborn (one who looks like a flour-dusted chicken or an infant from Pompeii) is sad-funny. Those conjoined emotions enhance each other. At the moment of rebirth, there is mystery, beauty, ugliness, grief … and, hopefully, a little laughter.

I suppose this could have been a lyric poem. It could have become a short story or a lyric essay. But like the foggy woman, it's caught in between. Here the prose poem hybrid feels more poem-like to me. I don't pour my words into a pre-conceived vessel. They form their own shape or genre as they gather their wits and coalesce. I don't really care how the finished piece is classified, but it makes it easier for publishing to have a label for it. The book in which this piece appears, *Stirring the Mirror,* is a collection of prose poetry and flash fiction. The book starts out on the more poetic side, then wobbles more toward flash fiction at the end. The pieces connected each to the next in a congenial, hybrid way.

Prose poetry invites the reader to travel far in a small space. Like lyric poetry, it's more of a core sample, unlike fiction's topographic map. For me, it's a playful yet serious way of getting to deeper themes, of excavating a bigger truth. Its simple, rectangular shape and short length (almost always a single page or under for my own prose poems) work well to create a small stage, a dungeon, a launching pad, a mirror, a window … or a closet holding a creation myth.

Mary A. Koncel

After the Weather

Yesterday a man was sucked out of an airplane over the blue-tipped mountains of Bolivia. He didn't cry "emergency." He didn't buzz the stewardess. He just dropped his fork, opened his mouth, and let the wind gather him inch by inch.

The other passengers agreed. This was real life, better than the movie or chicken salad. They leaned out of their seats, envying the man, arms and legs spread like a sheet, discovering raw air and the breath of migrating angels.

Below, an old peasant woman beat her tortilla. She never dreamed that above her a man was losing his heart. Perhaps she was a barren woman, and when he landed, she'd say, "Yes, this is my son, a little old and a little late, but still my son."

And the man, he thought of wind and flocks of severed wings, then closed his eyes and arched himself again. He didn't understand. His head began to ache. He understood Buicks, red hair, the smell of day old beer. But not these clouds, this new, white sunlight, or the fate of a man from Sandusky, Ohio.

Commentary

I wrote "After the Weather" a fairly long time ago. I had fallen asleep on the couch during the 11 o'clock news but woke up just after the weather report—hence the title of the poem—to a story about a man being sucked out of an airplane. Still in that semi-conscious sleep state, I sat up, trying to listen for more details that weren't forthcoming. Instead a beleaguered fender for a body shop commercial danced across the TV screen, and exhausted, I dozed back to sleep.

The next day I was hooked. Who was the man? Where was the airplane headed? Did he float like a leaf or drop like a can of tomato juice? I searched the newspapers looking for the story, found nothing, then began to wonder if, perhaps, I hadn't really heard the story but instead dreamt it, imposing dream on reality. Either way, so what! Such inviting ingredients for a prose poem—no beginning, no end, just the image of the man and all the possibilities.

"After the Weather" has modest ambitions—it doesn't take on a whole event but instead tries to capture the essence of it—in this case, the last moment or two in this poor man's life. For me, the tight contained box of the prose poem invites such focus. But what I find challenging about this form is how much I can fit into that box, how wide can I expand the lens, how I can rearrange and reconstruct the details. The prose poem encourages me to play, to surprise myself, to be impulsive and have fun. So even if the poem is intent on the man's final moments, it opens up to include not just him but the major characters around him.

Looking back, I think this poem works off some quiet tensions. First, its structure. On the one hand, it moves quickly from the man to the other passengers to the old peasant woman then back to the man. On the other hand, it was important to suspend the moment, to explore both the horror and the humor of this man's predicament. (How sad it would be if he just tumbles down to earth—The End!) So while the shifts from stanza to stanza provide momentum to the narrative, I also think they help to slow it down, to hold the man and the reader so that both can linger just a second or two longer.

Language, too, contributes to this tension. Yes, a man being sucked out of an airplane is not a lucky man—the inevitable is, of course, a dead man. Yet to soften the inevitable and, again, to suspend the moment, I wanted a mix of lines—short, direct reportage and longer, more luxurious ones—a juxtaposition that helps create the music which I think is so essential to the prose poem. Take the second stanza. The opening is reasonably straight-forward. But then comes,

"They leaned out of their seats, envying the man, arms and legs spread like a sheet, discovering raw air and the breath of migrating angels." There's something pretty being said, almost as good as the lyrics from a John Denver song. Finally, that bit of dialogue—something I love to include in my prose poems because it so often has such natural cadence. In this poem, the four syllable units as well as the repetition of "son" and "little" provide this music. At the same time, the old woman's words are both humorous and tender, giving life to the man at a point in the narrative when he should be meeting his end.

Gerry LaFemina

Thinking of You

I like to think of you since I think.
—Jaime Sabines

I like to think of you in the shower, not because I like to imagine your body naked, sheened with water (though I do), but because of how you sing in the spray songs I can't decipher.

I like to think of you at the table at work while I am at the table at work, our table like an unscrolled map of a continent I would cross on horseback if I must. There is a time difference at play. Every day I consult the almanac of your name.

I like to think of you in the waning minutes of light before full dark in the country where full dark still exists and how you become in that moment dusky, mysterious. Your earrings, the night's first stars.

I like to think of you writing this postcard in invisible ink, the one I turn over in my hands with my morning coffee, my morning scratch of the cat's head.

I like to think of you because I am when I think and I am more-than when I think of you. Now is not the time for a lesson on less-than thoughts.

Of course, you've heard such things before—guys almost like me are lined up on soup lines. They hunger. They thirst. I like to think of you so I can continue to go without.

Commentary

This prose poem started in a studio apartment on Manhattan's Upper West Side that I shared with a woman I was in love with and who loved me in her way. We both loved the prose poem. I was reading Jaime Sabines's *Weekly Diary and Poems in Prose & Adam and Eve* and was struck by the quote that became the epigraph. So much of love after all is how we think about the beloved, how we create biochemical trails that our thoughts keep taking, dopamine receptors turned on.

And what is the imagination but a type of thought?

It's an incantation, of course. The woman was incredibly self-conscious of her singing and dancing, and often would sing and dance in the apartment when I was gone. She had a great voice and moved gracefully, but still, it was often when I was gone that she really let loose. I could hear her, though, in the shower, her voice above the spray, muffled through the door. The nakedness I was interested in wasn't her body's nakedness, but the nakedness of unselfconsciousness.

We had this small table we'd sit at, like people at a chessboard, each of us writing or reading. And because my job was in Maryland and I kept a house there, that distance is implicit in the "continent" between us. My driving back and forth to her became riding "horseback." She would sometimes slip me a postcard into my bag before leaving or mail one to my house, so it was waiting for me. Once she gave me a blank one because she had nothing to say but she wanted me to have it anyway. It was at my desk where I would look at while drinking coffee. My cat, Tesla, on my lap. Our cat, Nigel, in the studio.

The poem, in other words, was trying to capture the distance and the proximity of our relationship. But it's also a meditation on the way we think about love, the way our thinking about love makes love happen, in some way. So riffed Descartes, "I think, therefore I am": "I like to think of you because I am when I think" but then I wanted to say something about love and the beloved: "and I am more-than when

I think of you." Let's face it, being in love makes us feel literally and figuratively more than ourselves. And that moment of loving "is not the time for a lesson on less-than thoughts." Because I sometimes felt insecure in our relationship, this last sentence felt particularly important. Really, this prose poem was my postcard to her, declaring my feelings.

Metaphor is at the heart of poetry, and my favorite prose poems engage the image in keen ways. Metaphor, too, is at the heart of how we talk about affairs of the heart. So each section of the poem is running its own metaphor: it's a prose poem composed of smaller prose poems. And how to end it.

The poem ends on the inadequacy of the relationship. Of the speaker himself who is like so many other men who are homeless: literally, whatever the studio was, it was a place where neither of us felt at home—she couldn't sing when she wanted, and I was chronically leaving and returning. There is also a sense that despite the hunger and thirst there was some sort of appetite, something necessary and deep in the bone, being satisfied.

As with all the prose poems I wrote during our time together, she read this one. I can't say anymore whether she liked it. We talked about prose poems a lot—hers, mine, and ones we admired. This poem wouldn't exist without her; more clearly, though, it wouldn't exist without the Sabines poem. The inspiration that comes from reading, from holding someone else's phrase and seeing what's possible for one's own work, that was the real delight. That's the dialogue of literature, one that I continue to eavesdrop on, and sometimes, join.

David Lehman

Mother Died Today

Mother died today. That's how it began. Or maybe yesterday, I can't be sure. I gave the book to my mother in the hospital. She read the first sentence. Mother died today. She laughed and said you sure know how to cheer me up. The telegram came. It said, Mother dead Stop Funeral tomorrow Stop. Mother read it in the hospital and laughed at her college boy son. Or maybe yesterday, I don't remember. Mama died yesterday. The telegram arrived a day too late. I had already left. Europe is going down, the Euro is finished, and what does it matter? My mother served plum cake and I read the page aloud. Mother died today or yesterday and I can't be sure and it doesn't matter. Germany can lose two world wars and still rule all of Europe, and does it matter whether you die at thirty or seventy? Mother died today. It was Mother's Day, the day she died, the year she died. In 1940 it was the day the Germans marched into Belgium and France and Churchill succeeded Chamberlain as Prime Minister. The telegram came from the asylum, the home, the hospital, the assisted-living facility, the hospice, the clinic. Your mother passed away. Heartfelt condolences. The price of rice is going up, and what does it matter? I'll tell you what I told the nurse and anyone that asks. Mother died today.

May 10, 2012

Commentary

"Mother Died Today" is in prose, because it begins with a prose sentence—"Mother died today," the first sentence in *The Stranger* by

Albert Camus. My mother died on May 10, 2009, which fell on a Sunday that year, Mother's Day. Ever since, I have observed my mother's passing twice each year, once on May 10 and once on Mother's Day. And it was in observance of her passing that I wrote this poem on May 10, 2012.

I began with a memory of the day when, as a college freshman reading the existentialists for French class, *The Stranger* was in my jacket pocket when I went to the hospital to visit my mother, there for a minor operation. The very brief opening paragraph of *The Stranger,* consisting of brief utterances and sentences fragments, with a pervasive air of indefiniteness, served as a model. My method was to repeat ("died today") and vary ("passed away"), to allow the rhythm of the prose to carry me forward, which it did—into the past. Dates have a way of imprinting themselves on my memory—I am fascinated by them—and the specific events that took place on May 10, 1940, are as I describe them in the poem. The Nazis launched their westward invasion. Churchill came to power. It was an unforgettable day in the lives of everyone in Europe and Great Britain, and that included my mother, who had not yet arrived in America. She was a refugee in London on May 10, 1940, having managed to escape from Nazi Austria after the Anschluss.

Isn't this how the mind works? And perhaps especially when in the icy grip of some overwhelming emotion? We associate freely; we repeat ourselves, and the repetitions can sometimes sound sinister, sometimes comic; we mix up time periods, with maybe some rueful awareness of current events; we make note of coincidences, because we suspect that they are not coincidences at all—that they cohere if only in some remote and secret realm. We end where we began, and the question that lingers after us can only be evaded, never satisfactorily answered.

Lesle Lewis

When "Towns, Cities, and Villages Disappeared from the Earth"

The afternoon falls away like a crack-in-the-glass.

The mind realizes itself and the wind wrecks the umbrella.

Never mind the world—but mind it too.

And allow yourself some regular old happiness and poems.

I like your poems a lot (so much in fact that you don't have to like mine).

Your poems are the master of "and' and the mistress of "this."

I met them in their jeep on a back road where I was walking.

They had with them an envelope with five hundred dollars on the front seat between them.

I know this because they showed it to me.

Commentary

I don't have conscious intentions for poems, but when I read what a poem has become I see what I have learned in the writing. Now I see in this poem that when I am having a hard time, when the afternoon falls away, I save myself by reading (and sometimes writing) poems. The poem addresses a particular poet I was reading and it also acknowledges how in walking (which might even work as a metaphor for reading) I come to realize things. Poems are people too. And the mystery of the envelope is revealed to me. I don't know how to make good line-break decisions so I use the sentence as my structure/form. Sometimes a sentence takes up two lines. The title of the poem comes from James Thurber's *The Last Flower.*

P. H. Liotta

The Blue Whale

Drifting on a river she could not control, the broken carcass of a blue whale came to our shores. By then, jaw already cracked from the prop-blade of another ship, she lingered too long at the surface, unable to feed. Struck by a tanker crossing from Angers to Providence, buoyed by the bulbous chin of the bow, the leviathan never knew what hit her. Water pressure kept the corpse in place until they entered Narragansett Bay. Dead a week already, she was gaffed and hooked and dragged alongside the pilot boat to Second Beach.

Back then, no one knew if she were male or female. "She" might glory in the sand while "he" grew fetid and fell away, waiting for dissection. The skeleton would be buried in the dunes, in secret, when it was done. Like the odd doctor in Marlow's darkness, who measures the crania of those who drift "out there" and "up the Congo," with caliper-like things, "in the interest of science." *Oh, I never see them come back,* he says.

By the time I get there, cubism has set in. A thousand faces circle the cadaver. The dead remains: a wishbone bent toward nothing, her inverted jawbone jabs at sky. Mist fizzles into rain. The organs splayed out in the drift sizzle like sound of crackling bacon. Each fleck of water slices at the desiccated blood. Thousands flock to thrill at absence. There's still enough to feel the loss. A river of baleen. A disembodied fluke.

Two days on, the ebb of human flotsam has washed clean. "He" and "she" are going now—into the gloam. A bulldozer grumbles in the downpour: a single beacon, tachistoscopic, flaming red. And when the three of us arrive, everyone and thing are gone. My daughter turns in wind and keeps on asking, *What does she look like? Why did she die?* Just face the order out to sea, the pictures of a floating world: the subject sees but never speaks. The way you fear the menace left unsaid—the natural convergence weighing down. You dream alone.

Out there, what difference between what stretches ahead and what is past. The Acropolis and Parthenon streaming into view. The ruined Balkans, hope and slaughter. Breadlines in St. Petersburg.

Kurds fleeing from the bombing runs. Head for the Kyrgiz steppe. See for yourself: the free spillage of Tajik blood or the chaos-order of the Taliban. The black sturgeon, up from Caspian depths, flashing through air. Diamond in darkness. Behold the nothing that is not there and the nothing that is.

I don't know about you. But for me, we're drifting still. I see the wreck of a whale, watch it going, going … like seals in the outer harbor, who tumble in brine and do their best ignoring death, like the one tied to the mast with wax in ears who was forced not to listen, what good could come in reading the runes of a ruined life? O lantern without bearer, you, too, are drifting, to spite your course.

Sachuest Point, Aquidneck Island

Commentary

"I drifted on a river I could not control," Rimbaud proclaimed with equal fragments of pride, despair, and willing loss in "Le bateau ivre." So much for poetic intent.

I am writing this from the place once named Yugoslavia. Last night at dinner, my companion Drago, an abdominal surgeon, turned to me and said, "So, you want to know about war?" I supposed that he was joking and did not anticipate his answer. He crossed the room and returned with a sheath of color negatives. Less dramatic, perhaps, than spilling a basketful of human ears onto the table, but by the end more stunning … I held the pictures to the light and saw arms torn from their shoulder sockets, shrapnel from a homemade mortar buried in a woman's skull, the back thigh and buttock of a child ripped away. What was left looked more like automaton than human being. I thought I would vomit. We were at his table, drinking wine, eating *pršut* with *Kackavalj* cheese. Hundreds of these pictures. He claimed to have performed three thousand operations during the war. "This is 'the enemy,'" he said. He was not talking about the artillery or gunfire, the mines. He meant the people he used to laugh and work with. He meant his former neighbors.

I am standing in the ash of Vukovar, in the ruins of the children's hospital, where graffiti on the wall proclaims, "We will slaughter you all!" Where their broken bodies were tossed into a mass grave only recently discovered near the stadium. The youngest was six months old. The empty hull of the place.

I am writing you from a place where you have never been. I could tell you how I thought a prose poem came to be. How I drank too much the night before, how there might have been a celebration for some forgotten end, or how, the morning after, I found myself composed by equal fragments of guilt and clarity. How I had seen a Scandinavian film titled *My Life as a Dog,* how the hero of the story, a young boy, spends his time in the barn, dreaming himself into a capsule alongside Laeke—the dog the Soviets launched into space in 1957. But that would be a lie. The blue whale came to Second Beach on the island where I live. A tanker hit the whale somewhere in the vicinity of Nova Scotia and traveled all the way to Narragansett Bay before the crew discovered they had been pushing a behemoth off their bow for days. After study and dissection, researchers learned the "specimen" was a young male, sixty-five feet in length.

What you name and what you fear are the order you compose. What I've written down is basically true, though there may well be no basic truth. So the river flows. With no control. The earth was salt before the ocean turned to tears.

Gian Lombardo

38

Oil & Water

The rope you hold begs the question: How to tie a noose and toss it over a branch? Put it over your head to see how it fits.

But before you can braid that deadly knot, someone grabs the other end and runs. You dig your heels in.

With the rope taut, that someone circles around you. You twirl, describing a smaller orbit to keep from being wrapped in the line. Soon the world's a queasy blur. Who will let go first?

Commentary

I've been using the *I Ching,* the ancient Chinese book of the divination, to wrestle with problems for most of my adult life. The elaborate ritual of throwing the yarrow sticks to come up with the lines of a hexagram empties mind and heart of everything, so that I'm able to view the problem with fresh eyes, using the text of the resulting hexagram as a guide to seeing the world anew.

I always had the desire to create a book entwined in some way with the *I Ching,* though I could never decide on its proper form. Then, a few years ago, I realized that a commentary on or the symbolism of each hexagram could generate (as the surrealists said) the flash of an image. I wanted to let that image, or a complex of images, illuminate the barest backbone of a narrative. I wanted to explore the nuances of creating stories by "throwing" images; to investigate what it takes to "see" and how one proceeds from perception to thought and feeling.

"Oil & Water," the 38th hexagram, is named *K'uei*—disunion, or mutual alienation. It represents, symbolically, fire (which tends to move upwards) over a marsh (whose waters tend to move downwards). This symbolism yields the interpretation that even where there's general agreement, there still may be diversity. In terms of its symbolic representation of family relationships, the hexagram can be seen as two sisters who live together but whose wills do not move in the same direction.

For the first thirty-seven hexagrams, the ability to see an image develop from the commentary or symbolism came easily. However, I became blocked by hexagram 38 because it let loose an avalanche of conflicting thoughts and emotions about my family. Instead of a "clearing," followed by a quasi-revelatory apperception, I became fixed on the apparition of my mother, who was suffering from Alzheimer's disease, and her sister, with whom she shared a two-family house. Steadfastly denying my mother's affliction, my aunt endeavored to care for her, sacrificing time with her own children, grandchildren and great-grandchildren. For twenty years, both sisters lived together after their husbands died, recreating the love—and accompanying conflicts and jealousies—of their childhood. As my mother's Alzheimer's progressed her behavior became more paranoid and confused; she became incoherent and withdrawn—a terrible burden for her sister who was exceedingly trusting, lively and sociable.

For weeks I approached *K'uei*'s text, rereading and rereading, yet nothing came. Finally, afraid the project might grind to a halt, I moved on to the next hexagram. Eventually, the process of working on other hexagrams provided the same "clearing" relief as the ritual of throwing the sticks. Every once in a while, I'd go back to the *K'uei,* until one time, out of the darkness, came an image from astronomy—that of a double sun (wherein two stars revolve around each other in close proximity). This image captured the essence of these two loving, strong-willed women. Going with that image, I likened the gravity that holds the two stars together (as well as the contra-acting centripetal force keeping them from colliding and fusing) to a rope. And from the rope, a noose. From that point on, the images fell in line in a way that allowed the possibility of a story of two people: one (or the other) decides to "check out" and one (or the other) attempts to keep the one (or the other) alive by pulling on the rope. They end up spinning each other around, locked as much by love as by their conflicting wills until one lets go—a letting go that makes us wonder whether it is a release of love or a refusal to serve.

"Letting go" represents, on another level, the process of relinquishing petty and major thoughts and feelings in order to be able to re-enter life again with eyes open. Considering all these layers of "letting go," I felt it more appropriate to change the title of the collection from *The Briefest Zoo in the Universe* to *Who Lets Go First.*

Robert Hill Long

Malpensa, Outbound

At this age, one starts at the end—held in the palm like a skein of burnt rope. No: a few hairs, finger-combed from the head while driving open-windowed from Nîmes to Uzés. Hairs trapped in the knuckles, released on a curve into the limestone canyon whose walls are flecked with swallows and swallow-shadows rising over the Citroen, downshifting toward river-flicker at canyon bottom.

Violet-green swallows, thirty years earlier, swooped to drink the ankle-breaking chill of the Roaring Fork River in Colorado. I couldn't afford the flight to my grandmother's deathbed two thousand miles east, so made the river her bed and waited there. Hateful, her coma; hateful, my impoverished distance, but I needed her death to make a poem she deserved. I stuck my head beneath frigid whitewater to start feeling, to stop feeling. Then finger-combed blond knots out, flicked them into water. Swallows touched down, a sip and gone; vainly I imagined them plucking a thread of me from the river, flying it east over the mountains. The river-canyon there, too, the sunlit wall over me, was limestone.

Whatever I pull from my head now is mixed with lime and ash. Somewhere near the Pont du Gard there must be—in a nest, I hope, glued to its Roman arches—at least one of my father's hairs from the second trip he made to France and leaned his sixty-something head out the Peugeot's window into the Rhone wind. Swallows can catch anything that flies, why not a hair from my father's head? No one had caught the fatal tracing, yet, in the yearly portrait of his bones. He was in France for his nephew's wedding in the stone crypt of the Huguenot temple: ancient vows in an ancient tongue. He danced with the bride in dry grass beneath the walls of a courtyard where a side of bull turned on an iron spit. In place of the groom's dead father, in a peach silk blazer, he maneuvers the bride past the bull, ash swirls round them. A last waltz, though none of us knew it yet, in the south of France.

And when his hair was brown, he shot up France in a nine-ton warplane, diving out of clouds to bomb railyards, convoys. He strafed a train, a freight car started frothing like a washing machine with too much soap: the German officers' winter champagne supply, meant to tide them through months of tactical retreat with their own memories (August weddings on the Moselle's vineyard steeps, anniversaries on a Danube ferry) intact and warm. Another day, drunk on a chateau roof in Reims, he plunged through a skylight onto the general's table, shouted "Dinner is served!" and passed out. His mother wrote up his exploits in the hometown paper. He caught a pair of soldiers fleeing on a motorcycle and buzzed them from behind at treetop level to "give them a squirt"—a stitching of .50-caliber puffs alongside to scare them home. They panicked and gunned the bike into eight converging streams of steel—*perfect harmonization,* gunnery school lingo—and became human champagne bubbles. This story he never told his mother, or his wife. He told me only when he knew he would never rise from bed again.

A thread holds it together, this tapestry in the skull's lime temple. There's no perspective, the gentlest tug unravels its borders. It's crowded: a fine old woman dying in a hospital bed, her son ditto alongside, plus a third, empty bed I'm fleeing—I'm that tiny figure speeding an Italian autostrada, Citroen flying, leaving a tinier, younger self behind to cry in a Colorado river. A train bursts into champagne, a bull waltzes with smoke, heady mix of bubbles and gunfire. Its ashen ends are knotted to my scalp, its top corner is in an outgoing swallow's beak, unweaving, flying backwards out of our story to glue a few bricks on a Roman aqueduct.

In this Airbus awaiting clearance outside Milan, I'm impatient to fly, to finish this journey I did not wish to end. Hateful seatbelt, armrests tight and cold as hospital bedrails. Was this impatience wrung from a vaporized motorcycle, foretold on that gunstick between my father's legs? Where's the explanation? In those clouds over the runway whose destiny is snow, snow whose future is a river. In a few knuckles-worth of hair released in a country we all left yesterday. The tower signals *Go.* Avalanche of whine, forward thrust, liftoff, my head pinned against the headrest—as it ought to be.

Commentary

I ceased a long relationship with a famous legal poison on Easter seven years ago, some three decades after I imagined I could handle it for the long term, despite what Tom Lux used to say about writers and alcohol. Owing to its intimate not to say parasitical intertwinings with the writing process—mostly with revision, but what's the difference when life depends on forms of denial, deception and self-medication?—I took leave from writing, too, seven years ago. The joys of sobriety, emergent then ever-expanding, were not worth risking for what I used to rationalize as a discipline, accomplished late at night when everyone was asleep or dead. Like being a jet pilot who plunged over and over into the ocean, determined to keep flying through submarine darkness to seek something undiscoverable any other way, something unbearable in the light of day. A sick discipline in retrospect: a submergence that involved a little drowning each time, a narcosis that took on its own personality over decades of practice.

I haven't worked on writing poems or prose poems or books since. A few have arrived as Keats thought they should—as naturally as leaves from a tree. Gifts, not struggles with self-induced darknesses or crippling angels. At this point in recovery, "*Malpensa, Outbound*" more than anything embodies the unhappiness of discovering in one life after another the same patterns of disillusionment and doom, memento mori everywhere. It dates from the first decade of this century, like a lot of other works in short prose and poetry I expect never to collect, a literary relic from a life where everything was defined—or should I say distilled—in relation to death and memory, to history and futility and forgetting. Those fumes have burned off by now. Maybe its images and sentences have some value apart from the ways I drugged and killed off moments of my life to acquire them, or as a warning about the occupational hazards of a writing life.

Morton Marcus

The Canary Islands

"What islands are those?" I asked the first mate.

We had passed several treeless, rolling islands, wind-ruffled yellow under the pale blue sky, each without houses or any sign of human habitation.

"The Canaries," he replied, unshaven, his black sweater grimy at collar and cuff.

"All that wheat," I said. "Who plants it?"

"Those are the canaries," he said again. "Hundreds of thousands of them fly here several times a year and bunch together on the swells."

I had taken passage on the only ship available during the hellish war, a Yugoslav tanker, all rust and shuddering metal. I never knew its cargo: the crew sneered whenever I approached.

"You can't be serious," I said to the first mate, still staring at the island. He didn't reply, but spit on the deck near my shoes, and lumbered away.

I leaned on the railing, peering at the landfalls. They certainly could have been birds, birds who sought refuge from the world's murderousness, flying from everywhere on the planet at appointed times to huddle together and be revitalized.

The next day they were gone, and I didn't ask about them again. But I still imagine them, those temporary islands, suddenly coming apart in the night, separating into hundreds of thousands of wings scattering to the seven continents, where they fall like pieces of moonlight on the houses of the sleepers, silent, unseen, neither substance nor shadow, yet more than a possibility, a presence, really, that periodically departs from our lives but always returns.

Commentary

A friend who is also a successful novelist, recently wrote me a troubled letter, responding to "The Canary Islands." His question showed the novelist's allegiance to the methods and manners, as well as the mind-set, of the prose fiction writer, an allegiance that was made clear when he prefaced his comments by saying that "as a novelist" he "kept going off in habitual directions" as he read the poem.

At first, he said, he assumed that I was talking about the real Canary Islands, and even though he could grudgingly accept the islands being composed of birds, he had more difficulty with the idea that canaries gather together in floating colonies, since that was just not true. So I was writing about "symbolic or fantasy canaries," right? But what were they symbolic of? And if they were "a presence that departs from our lives but always returns," what could that presence be? And what about the narrator's part in this piece? What is "that hellish war," and what is the reason for his leaving it? Why does the crew sneer at the narrator when he asks about the cargo, and why don't they tell him what it is? Why does the first mate spit near the narrator's shoes? Why are they all so contemptuous: what has the narrator done to them?

These are good questions, but they're to be asked of another genre. They are the concerns of the practitioner of realistic fiction, who constantly questions which scenes to develop and which not, and who is obsessed with ferreting out the reasons behind every detail and character action.

Such questions do not apply to "The Canary Islands," which, because it is symbolic and essentially absurdist, does not seek to explain the world in the same way the realistic novel does, but in its metaphorical approach assumes that events and actions are ultimately unexplainable—that life is a mystery and that the rational questions we ask about it are, in the end, unanswerable. Therefore, details are presented not only to enrich the atmosphere of the piece but to prod readers into pursuing their own sense, symbolically speaking, of what the cargo is, why the crew is hostile to the narrator, and to elaborate on the implications hopefully resonating from each detail.

And what about this nameless narrator? Should readers consider him a rounded fictional character? Since he is a first-person narrator, can they trust him? And how much of what he says may be a phantom of his imagination? One of the few traits the narrator exhibits is an understandable desire to get away from that "hellish war," a hostile event that is reflected in the actions of the ship's crew. The crew and the war are part and parcel of a general antagonism that the narrator opposes, or, more accurately, to which he is placed in opposition. Antagonists and protagonist: it's as simple as that; and the protagonist, I hope, emerges as an Everyman confronting an archetypal situation. Out of this predicament, the narrator envisions the canaries as a revitalizing impulse he needs to believe in which will result in the tenuous re-establishment of peace and harmony. That is what the canaries' "presence" represents to him.

The canaries, then, are metaphorical, and metaphor, not cause-and-effect motivation, is the center of the piece. In fact, this poem works like many of my others: an image or metaphor presents itself in my imagination and I pursue its meaning. The idea behind the pursuit is that no metaphor or image is accidental or random: there is a reason I thought it in the first place, and the attempt to find or, more probably, to catch a glimpse of this reason is the impetus behind the pursuit, no matter how outlandish the original image or metaphor might be.

The prose poem has many alluring features, but what makes it unique to me is the tension that holds it together in an excited force field, so to speak, created by the attempt to combine the antithetical elements of narrative prose intentions and poetic techniques. This tension has much to do with the narrative's impulse to expand on one side and poetry's compulsion to condense on the other. This force field occurs where prose and poetry meet—where the narrative faces the lyrical head-on.

Peter Markus

Light

When he wasn't working, on his days off, his father liked to spend his day outside, in the shingle-bricked, single-car garage, tinkering with his '52 Chevy Bel Air: a stoop-roofed, two-tone junker he bought off a drunk buddy of his, a fellow hot metal man by the name of Lester Litwaski, for a fifth of whiskey and a scrunched-up dollar bill. There were days when his father wouldn't take five minutes to come into the house to eat a hot lunch. Days like these, his mother would send him outside into the garage with a cold corned beef sandwich and an apple, and his father would stop working only long enough to wolf down this food, his hands gloved with grease and dust, before ducking back under the Chevy's jacked-up back axle. Sometimes his father would fiddle around past midnight, his bent-over body half-swallowed by the open mouth of the hood, his stubby, blood-crusted fingers guided by the halogen glow of a single bare light-bulb hanging down like a cartoon thought above his hunchbacked silhouette. Sometimes he would stay up late and watch his father's shadow stretch like a yawn across the walls of the garage. And in the darkness of his room he would sit, silently, on the edge of the bed, by the window, and wait for that moment when his father raised up his hand, as if he were waving, as if he were saying goodbye, and turned off the light.

Commentary

When I was in graduate school struggling to write short fiction, I was heavily under the influence of writers such as Raymond Carver and Richard Ford, and under their influence I was writing stories that anyone trying to write short stories might write. The bulk of these short stories or attempts at short stories were conventionally long and conventionally written, heavy on character and plot and not as much concerned with language or given over to the lyrical impulse.

All of this changed, one day, with the writing of a short piece (let's call it what it is, a prose poem) called "Light." But it wasn't always a prose poem, to begin with; it was, instead, nothing more than a flashback paragraph early on—if memory serves, somewhere in the vicinity of page three of a thirty-three page story—in a story that simply, for whatever reason—for reasons obvious to me now (I hadn't yet found the language or the cadence that was mine to write with)—was floundering on its way toward its own eventual death in workshop. Lucky for me I was lucky enough to be working at the time with Stuart Dybek, himself a master of the short-short form, who was kind enough to praise my much too long fiction (no matter how lame and limited it might have been) for its mood and strong sense of place. It's true, in this early work, as there is in much of my later work, there was smoke and smokestacks and just enough whiskey to keep things leaning toward the dramatic. I think that's what Stu saw in this early work: smoke and smokestacks, if not actual fire. But back to "Light." The story, as I said, was struggling. It was, as we say in the dirty river town where I'm from in Michigan, dead in the water. It had no or little light to it. I would read it over and over and knew that it just wasn't right. I should have ditched the whole story after running it aground through its first couple of drafts. But I was young and stubborn and working-class so I kept writing and revising and re-reading through it, working to rub off the rust. That's when, at some point in the rewriting/rewiring process, I experienced a breakthrough moment, when I found myself returning to page three where I was once again rereading that passage that began with the words, "When he wasn't working, on his days off, his father liked to spend his day outside, in the shingle-bricked, single-car garage, tinkering with his '52 Chevy Bel Air: a stoop-roofed, two-tone junker he bought off a drunk buddy of his, a fellow hot metal man by the name of Lester Litwaski, for a fifth of whiskey and a scrunched-up dollar bill."

There are still things about this poem in prose, this boxy little paragraph, there are still things about the language of this world, that I find troublesome, or I am troubled, at times, by how I am saying my saying. But for the most part, even now, over twenty-five years later (I was a mere twenty-five at the time that I wrote it), I find that I can still live with this piece of writing as a prose poem, or as a short-short story, which is what I think, in the end, it is. At that moment—I speak about this moment often with my students, the moment when I felt myself becoming a writer—I cut every word, and every page, around that one short single paragraph on page three of that thirty-three page story.

I'd never before made such a severe and drastic cut to anything I'd written up until that point in my writerly life; in the years since, it's true, I have hit delete on entire book-length manuscripts, have thrown a laptop into the river, have fed pages and pages of failed poems to my backyard fire pit. But when I found "Light" buried in so much dim and muddied darkness, it was a moment when I realized that sometimes a single, simple short passage can contain, and can radiate, casting a shadow much bigger than the thing itself. I can't help but think of William Carlos Williams here and his insistence on "No ideas but in things." Small things. Ordinary things. A red wheelbarrow glazed with rainwater. A plum in the freezer. A pile of cinders in which shine the broken pieces of a green bottle. A father alone in a garage, being watched by his son, a boy who loves him, even if he doesn't feel that he knows him, waiting for the moment when his father raises up his hand, as if he were waving, as if he were saying good-bye, and turns off the light.

Michael Martone

The Mayor of the Sister City Talks to the Chamber of Commerce in Klamath Falls, Oregon

"It was after the raid on Tokyo. We children were told to collect scraps of cloth. Anything we could find. We picked over the countryside; we stripped the scarecrows. I remember this remnant from my sister's obi. Red silk suns bounced like balls. And these patches were quilted together by the women in the prefecture. The seams were waxed as if to make the stitches rainproof. Instead they held air, gasses, and the rags billowed out into balloons, the heavy heads of chrysanthemums. The balloons bobbed as the soldiers attached the bombs. And then they rose up to the high wind, so many, like planets, heading into the rising sun and America …"

I had stopped translating before he reached this point. I let his words fly away. It was a luncheon meeting. I looked down at the tables. The white napkins looked like mountain peaks of a range hung with clouds. We were high above them on the stage. I am yonsei, the fourth American generation. Four is an unlucky number in Japan. The old man, the mayor, was trying to say that the world was knit together with threads we could not see, that the wind was a bridge between people. It was a hot day. I told these beat businessmen about children long ago releasing the bright balloons, how they disappeared ages and ages ago. And all of them looked up as if to catch the first sight of the balloons returning to earth, a bright scrap of joy.

Commentary

I started with the historical fact of Japanese balloon bombs and how thousands of them did actually make it across the Pacific. One went as far as Omaha. The hope of Japan was that the explosives would ignite forest fires. Some did, and the threat of those fires created the first squads of the famous "smoke jumpers" of fire suppression. One bomb did kill six, five children and one adult, a Sunday school class having a picnic in Bly, Oregon, 50 miles east of Klamath Falls. The only fatalities caused by any of the 9,000 plus balloons released. So there was this little bit of wonder and horror to begin with. I think the rest of the story is about (like the bombs themselves) the specific gravity of weightlessness, the heft of spoken language, its invisible propellant, its return to earth. The story is about the distortions of translations, censorship and editing, glossing and inflection. The balloons were gas-filled. Their locomotion provided by the wind. The story is about speech and a story spoken, intercepted, interpreted and misinterpreted, how it drifts around that room, searching for a landing, a target. We think, we wish, we hope language wants to connect, hopes to connect, connects. A story is collaboration between the author and the audience. Meaning is made in tandem. Perhaps, when I wrote this piece, this was my take on the new ideas emerging from another continent and "in the air," new theories about the imprecision of language, its deconstruction, its slipperiness, and the meaning of meaning in general. But for me the main drama is the way a beautiful, magical picture of this wondrous contraption (the balloon and the story of the balloon) and the construction of its construction is presented. For me it is how narrative is sent out on a lyrical mission to connect and shorten the distance, draw people and peoples closer, mend and stitch together, while, at the same time, the prose has this other bearing. It contains this invisible and preposterous horror of its subliminal message that only is demonstrated when it does hit the mark. The connection is a site of destruction. It is finally, I think, about the power of metaphor and the powerlessness of metaphor expressed at the exact same moment.

Kathleen McGookey

Ordinary Objects, Extraordinary Emotions

Dear Kathleen McGookey, Thank you for submitting your deceased mother's eyeglasses, straw fishing hat she wore as a child, and vial of four wisdom teeth for the Grand Rapids Public Museum's juried Day of the Dead exhibition "Ordinary Objects, Extraordinary Emotions." We carefully examined your loved one's belongings, but found they weren't quite what we were looking for. We received 7,562 items, with eyeglasses, hearing aids, dentures, and pipes topping the list. In fact, we considered commissioning an installation composed entirely of these articles, but as most people wanted their property returned, logistics overwhelmed us. While the selection committee sympathizes with the universal plight of how to dispose of emotionally charged artifacts, we regret we cannot take them into our collection, even temporarily. However, we wanted you to know your materials made it to the final round of consideration and the committee read your cover letter with interest. When they learned you still have your mother's blonde braids, cut off when she was twelve, her blue strapless prom dress, and perfect plaster reproductions of her feet, made when she was fitted for orthopedic shoes, the committee felt you did not submit your best objects. We are returning them in the postage-paid mailer you provided, and we wish you the best of luck placing them elsewhere.

Commentary

I'm grateful for the prose poem's ability to borrow characteristics of other kinds of prose, and to wear those borrowed clothes as a disguise when it ventures into the country of readers. In my case, I borrowed the form of a rejection letter. When a reader expects one thing (a straightforward rejection letter) and the prose poem delivers something oddly different (deceased mother's eyeglasses? vial of wisdom teeth?), a little chill runs down my spine.

I hope it's not just me.

Imagine what the prose poem might do as an encyclopedia entry or personal ad or recipe or horoscope or fairy tale or fable or instruction manual or permission slip or memo or advice column or legal brief or prayer or dictionary definition or....

A rejection letter's form provided a container for a difficult topic and made it possible for me to write about my mother's death in a way that surprised me. This poem arrived after I had already written many, many heartfelt elegies. Writing this poem was fun, which I didn't expect, given the subject and the absurd details that I could hardly talk about as I went through my mother's belongings: what in the world should I do with her glasses? or her prom dress? or, yes really, her braids? The poem came in a rush, nearly writing itself with those well-worn, detached phrases—"not quite what we were looking for," "best of luck placing them elsewhere"—that I'd read thousands of times. But something pivotal shifted when I took charge of the rejection. As I wrote, my feelings veered from giddy to sad and back again: laughter occasionally bubbled up in my throat while tears stung my eyes.

Campbell McGrath

Rifle, Colorado

I doubt they were used to strangers in the Rifle Café, wrapping their sausage in pancakes a little after dawn. I think the earnest woman frying eggs and the girl in the cowboy hat tracing her finger though spilled flour were mother and daughter. I doubt the lined man drinking bourbon at the bar was either father or brother. I don't know where the guides would lead their parties to hunt for bighorn and whitetail that day. I don't know how often they came to the café, or what they thought about, or what they ate. I don't know what their names were, where they lived, whether their families raised cattle or horses or stayed in bed in the morning.

I do know that there were cowboy hats and dirty orange workmen's gloves, the coffee was strong, the pancakes were good, Main Street was gravel, the river ran by, the sun rose just as we got there, night left the Rockies reluctantly, snow and timber diminished in daylight, the mountains emerged slowly with dawn—high country in winter is beautiful and lonely.

Commentary

This is the first or second prose poem I ever wrote, in the spring of my freshman year in college, at the University of Chicago, in 1981. The previous autumn I had driven across the country for the first time, with my friend Mike, in a car he had acquired with a fake driver's license from a driveaway auto-transhipment company in New York City, due for delivery a week later in Los Angeles. Growing up in the east I knew little about the west, and the poem vividly expresses my youthful amazement at pretty much everything we encountered en route. This and another poem about that same drive, "Silt, Colorado," were the first poems I ever had published—in the *Ohio Review*—and later appeared in my first book, *Capitalism,* in 1990; out of print for a long time, they will be included in my volume of new and selected poems, *Nouns & Verbs,* due from Ecco Press in 2019, making them the only poems of this long-ago era to have stood the test of time.

I have always been drawn to poetry as a documentary medium, and the capacious prose poem is well suited to accommodate landscape and narrative, social detail and historical exposition. This poem, with its western idiom, derives from a tradition that includes Gary Snyder, Jim Harrison, and James Wright, although, reading it now, it seems clear that Hemingway's Nick Adams stories had also seeped into the groundwater. I've never been certain why the dreamy, surrealist model came to dominate the American prose poem. Despite some remarkable examples of the genre (such as James Tate's canonical "Good Time Jesus"), they too often confine their exploration of human experience to claustrophobic interiors, and flatten language into absurdist tomfoolery. Dreams are not the only kind of journey for which the prose poem provides an ideal form—here's hoping that future generations of American poets will continue to voyage outside of themselves, as well as within.

Jay Meek

Travel Notes

I remember Cully; this is what happened there. As the captain turned our launch toward the dock, it was raining. In the rain, the Alps were blue. A man and woman sat together in front of the patisserie and watched a train passing on the hillside, toward Montreux. Seeing a chestnut tree in flower, I could hear everything thrum with the voice of its own kind, like that one tree in the rain, or even the most singular of poems, as it sounds. After we docked, a man and woman got off, but no one waved and no one met them. Then a man in blue uniform drew our gangway onto the deck, and we pulled away. There was nothing more. I made a note of how life shimmered in the town.

We need poems to help us change, and to ease our knowing. Not that a poem should assume more than we know, but allow what we do not know; that it might give to our weaknesses; that it might take us in confidence; that it might enact itself in us; that it might raise us out of ourselves. Even nights when we take it lovingly in our hands, and ease it of its sound, the poem we give our breath to is already assured beyond changing; it is a record of movement accomplished, of hope followed through into knowing. Of flawed perfections. Of conditional joy.

Yes, I was at Cully, and I'll remember it not only for its resonance and the rain but the pleasure I felt in discovering that whatever else it does, a poem will always make the sound of a poem. By this, it exempts itself from its own being, to hold us in mildness and quiet. Reading it, we can be at our best, without apology, and bear our lives in its song.

Commentary

In Michael Benedikt's introduction to *The Prose Poem: An International Anthology,* he voices an essential premise of the genre, concerning its "need to attend to the priorities of the unconscious. This attention to the unconscious, and to its particular logic, unfettered by the relatively formalistic interruptions of the line break, remains the most immediately apparent property of the prose poem." But I believe the prose poem is no less capable—and surely more capacious and unabashed than the lineated poem—of presenting, of representing, heightened states of consciousness. Dressed-down and even at times unassuming, the prose poem has become our causal lyric.

Rosmarie Waldrop speaks of wanting to introduce "*inside*" the prose poem the silences that frame verse poems: "I cultivate cuts, discontinuity, leaps, shifts of reference. 'Gap gardening', I call it." A prose poem gathers and extends, not exclusively by image or by syntax, and its measure is not the margin—or the simultaneous course through time and space that the verse poem weaves—but what goes on inside. In place of line and stanza, the prose poem depends upon tone and syntax, particularly for lightness; for it absorbs material much more voraciously than does a verse poem, simply to find its sufficiency and scale. So much to plant, so little time for rest.

"Travel Notes" began as jottings I wrote on a passenger boat making coastal stops on Lake Geneva from Lausanne west to a village on the French border. But it is also a passage through reflections, in which objects flicker in a consciousness that depends on them and declares them, a roll call of the ordinal and familiar—the launch, patisserie, chestnut tree—as each in turn "selves," to use Gerard Manley Hopkins' glorious verb. So, too, a poem is a record of its own making, a registry of its importances, that travels to the heart of each new reader. If it has its end in the writer, it goes out to find its best reader, in whom it lives a while. However different poems might be from one another, however individual we insist they be, they take part in the common experience of "poem" and by virtue of this become exempt from a singularity and strangeness.

Every poem unavoidably resonates with other poems of its kind, as Williams's "By the Road to the Contagious Hospital" does with Wordsworth's "I Wander Lonely as a Cloud." Sometimes, one poem might address other works across generations, as "Travel Notes" means to do by its gesture to Edward Thomas's great poem of motion and consciousness, "Adelstrop." Although some prose poems could otherwise have been verse poems, and some might in fact have begun as verse poems, what is remarkable is that often enough a prose poem cannot be said in any other way. I suspect that such "gap gardening" as "Travel Notes" contains, and such overt statements as it makes, would not have been easily possible in a lineated poem, without some degree of preciosity.

I admire the prose poem for its ability to face readers head on, an attitude less often found in verse poems, and I admire the ease with which a prose poem moves through time. Lineated poems are essentially spatial constructions; motion is at the heart of the prose poem. In "Travel Notes," I made a record of movement through a landscape, but also through an idea, its burden of distance expressed in the phrasing itself, in its cadences, silences, and sounds. But whether a poem is lineated or not, I believe that poems do give their readers the chance to be at their best, when in a consumer culture they are so often taken at something less, and that in reading poems that go all out, or mean to, readers needn't apologize for giving their best, or for asking it of themselves.

Shivani Mehta

This Is How I Learned About Regret

I was born with a detachable eye. My mother taught me to care for it, to pluck my eye from its socket so I could clean it. Most days after school, my brothers and sisters played with my eye, flicking it back and forth across the kitchen floor like a marble. Sometimes my mother made them give it back. Sometimes I searched for days before I found my eye in a bag of frozen peas, or in the pocket of my sister's sweater stuck to a half-chewed mint. Afterwards I sat at the kitchen table, polished my eye with a rag dipped in beeswax, the way my mother taught me. Back then only my family knew about my detachable eye but now things are different. Now I date a man who takes long showers. Sometimes I join him, my eye resting in a soap dish on the bathroom vanity. I cling to his wet body, my head on his shoulder, watching my eye watching us, like it belongs to someone else.

Commentary

I've loved jigsaw puzzles since I was a kid. The color and texture of the thick cardboard pieces between my fingers, smooth on the surface, rough and sharp-edged. I love the sound they make when I gather a few pieces in my hand, like the clicking of mah-jongg tiles. Over many years of doing jigsaw puzzles I've developed a methodical approach. First, I sort through the pieces looking for the end, or border pieces. Once I have these I spend some time constructing the puzzle border.

Somewhere during the process of writing a poem I begin to think of it as a jigsaw puzzle. I have some images, some phrases that I begin to think—hope—might come together and form a poem. The detachable eye in "Regret" was a cardboard puzzle piece, just as the mother in the poem was a piece of the puzzle. As the poem moves through various drafts, each draft becomes the box filled with messy pieces—other images, stray thoughts, sounds, etc—all offering an alternative version of the poem. That's where the poem and jigsaw puzzle begin to differ. In the end, there's only one correct jigsaw puzzle but there could be many versions of a poem. Though sooner or later, and in my case, later, you have to choose one. But eventually, I go back to the box of puzzle pieces and what didn't make it into one poem might appear in the next. Every puzzle is different.

Every poem is different. But the process is always the same. Each beginning requires a leap of faith, a belief that through the sorting, rotating, trying and discarding, the words will somehow coalesce to form a poem. When I press the last puzzle piece into place I'm always struck with a multitude of feelings—satisfaction, awe, gratitude. As well, I'm a little bit sorry that it's over.

Christopher Merrill

Notes for a Dance

The trees move into the holding place, eyes open, trunk and leaves, hundreds of poisoned apples scattered over hallowed ground, scrutinized by a flightless bird and all the aunts covering for the woman who slipped away. One story ended, and then another. And then? The moon shone through the plume rising from a volcano. The thief was rolled up in a rug and tossed overboard. Our guide declared a truce. Pause. Eyes closed. Say we were fluent in the language of turn and counterturn, fall and recovery, and then we weren't. Exchange this bag of gold for lessons in the logic of touch, without which each tree stands alone. What can you see, bent double at the waist, but bodies in motion, canoes filling with water, tattoos of flowers on her arms and legs? Eyes everywhere, if you can trust it. Wind equals touch in the cloud canopy: another galaxy to explore.

Commentary

Chance operations, slips of the tongue, random instructions, overheard bits of dialogue—these are some of the ways in which a poem begins for me, whether in traditional meters, nonce forms, free verse, or prose. "Notes for a Dance" was inspired by a cultural diplomacy mission to Cartagena, Colombia, where I collaborated with three American poets, members of the Bebe Miller Company, and young artists from the Colegio del Cuerpo to create a performance piece for dance and voice. The poets' first task was to describe the dancers' improvisations, finding language for movements discovered on the fly, and then to transcribe the dancer's words for what was in their minds as they twirled and leapt, spun and dropped to the floor of the semi-enclosed stage, changing positions and partners in the tropical heat: trees and leaves, birds and canoes. Some of the choreographer's directions—*Eyes open, Pause, Eyes closed*—found their way into this prose poem, along with one dancer's memorable phrase, *the logic of touch,* which is, of course, the logic of love, fulfilled and unrequited, lost and found. What emerged from my fevered jottings, then, was a sort of essay on the pleasures and perils of collaboration, which demands a level of trust commensurate with love. The dancers were exquisite, and my heart was breaking when they formed a circle at the end.

Robert Miltner

Wolf Dancing Is Back

No way you can stop fox-trotting on the back of a moving fox, not with its fur red as a Spanish Rioja wine, its tail like a frightened dust mop, its ears as pointed as folded French dinner napkins and that zany snout as conical as a megaphone. But wait: you pirouette on the xylophone of its spine, hold out your equilibrium arms as if the fox is a small coach or wagon and you're driving a team of matched Belgian draft horses at a nightlight-sized town's carnival. But wait: when you look down you realize this isn't a fox: it's a large black wolf, a dark nocturnal canine disguised as a vixen. No way you can suppress your joy at disco dancing on the back of a racing wolf. But wait: it begins to transform again: now it becomes a gray Irish wolfhound. A red Irish setter. A red wheelbarrow. What's next: a crayon-yellow cheetah or an ocelot? No way you can catch your breath break dancing at sixty miles per hour on the back of a rapid mammal that once answered to the name Reynard.

Commentary

Prose poetry is a genre in motion. Whether it is Gaspard de la nuit walking home from work, a cast-iron airplane taking flight, or a party train, prose poems rarely sit still like good dogs: how else could they make literary history?

Translation is a form of motion, from one language to another, from one genre to another and back again, or from one form of art to another, if ekphrastic. The origin of this prose poem was an interactive project at the Akron Art Museum between Buried Letter Press and the Melissa Stern *Talking Cure* exhibition that involved a writing workshop for the community and a reading by the workshop instructors of their ekphrastic responses to selected works from *Talking Cure.* "Wolf Dancing is Back" was written in reaction to Stern's drawing *Dancer/Wolf.* I was attracted to the way the piece was still when displayed on the gallery wall, yet seemed visually to be in motion within the composition itself. The tension between stillness and motion in the drawing echoes the balance on the page between the weight of prose and the lightness of poetry. The challenge in the writing of this prose poem was not just how to set the figures of the dancer and the fox in motion when placing the two within a single frame, but how to accelerate that motion once it had begun.

Transformation is another form of motion, for art draws from the mimetic world to create a world of fantasy. Fox to wolf to dog to cat and back to fox is like the genre-shifting interplay in the movement from prose to poem to prose, and can include the use of inventory for range and width and depth. The listing of Spain, Belgium, Ireland and France evokes European traditions of animal transformations and beast fables, represented by the allusion to the French Reynard fox stories. Russell Edson was the great fabulist in this vein: beast fables with a monkey in an oven, fish leaping up a staircase, a taxi that becomes a flock of yellow butterflies that reassemble back into a taxi. Edson's attraction to surrealism demonstrates his sense of play when the motion of his imagination crossed over from what is real to what exists beyond the real. In "Wolf Dancing is Back" I was drawn to the absurdity—a dimension of surrealism—of the narrative subject in the poem standing and dancing while riding a fox. I chose to locate the speaker as a plural wherein the "you" is concurrently the single reader, collective readers, and the self-reflective interior voice of the speaker—an impossibility posited as if both possible and also impossible, as absurd and also surreal, as both "no way" and yet "but wait."

Prose poetry is double, dual, defying singularity in favor of the multiple. So despite the title's word play, and despite its very impossibility, wolf dancing has not only always existed, it's now back in fashion.

Naomi Shihab Nye

His Life

I don't know what he thinks about. At night the vault of his face closes up. He could be underground. He could be buried treasure. He could be a donkey trapped in the Bisbee Mine, lowered in so long ago with pulleys and belts, kicking, till its soft fur faded and eyes went blind. They made donkeys pull the little carts of ore from seam to seam. At night, when the last men stepped into the creaking lift, the donkeys cried. Some lived as long as seventeen years down there. The miners still feel bad about it. They would have hauled them out to breathe real air in the evenings, but the chute was so deep and they'd never be able to force them in again.

Commentary

Prose poems invite us to make dramatic or delicately *odd leaps into the deep*—with no extensive build-up, prefacing or afterwards. I admire their directness. I admire their faith in us—that we may, if lucky, if similarly seized, follow their meanderings into some compelling region. In "His Life" I stare at a person I should know very well but don't, then (for relief?) dive into the old mine at Bisbee, Arizona, which I had recently visited, remembering what the ex-miner, now tour guide, told our group after we plied him with questions (tears clouded his eyes and he brushed them away). After the piece is over, I ruminate about lives, whether animal or human, spent in tied-up situations, but do I have to spell that out? No, no, no!

There is something infinitely satisfying in the blocky shape of the prose poem, after all the angularity and spaciousness of the more vertical poetry form. Prose poems are a refreshment, an oasis by the long reading highway. Entrances and exits are clearly marked. It is easy to feel engaged.

The prose-poem shape also suggests pockets and tables. It is curious how comforted I feel simply to see one popping up somewhere. I am restored to that brief time in first grade when we were invited (by our surly teacher, in my own case) to "make paragraphs"—once we had mastered the tricky art of the "sentence." What a wonder that was! The simple linkage of lines into a satisfying little house-shapes with windows and doors, dots and doormats ... all my school-life I was waiting to be invited to make "a paragraph" again. But it was never enough for anybody.

John Olson

Kierkegaard at Home Depot

I lie in my hospital bed dreaming of Laputa. The longer you live, the more your personal life becomes a conjunction, a sprocket of spectacular wizardry. Experience is always blind. Reflection gives it eyes. Grommets and morphine.

Or a little leisure, at least. A little idleness now and then goes a long way toward understanding silica, its chemistry and zigzags, its charm and tetrahedral coordination. I don't understand the scorn toward the semicolon, or the literary. Leaves bob and toss lightly in the rain, rejecting minimalism, espousing Proust.

Why does anyone write poetry? The intentions of the accordion are implicated in its folds. Imagine, for instance, Søren Kierkegaard at a Home Depot. He fondles a pair of self-adjusting slip joint pliers with a red handle and thinks that religious belief ought to be based on a strenuous exertion of will, but that the existence of God cannot be proved.

A voice over the loudspeaker announces a sale on halogen pendants and polished brass ceiling lights. What is it, he wonders, to be God's chosen? Is it to have denied in one's youth all the wishes of youth in order to have them fulfilled with great labor in old age?

If we did not have consciousness of the eternal and if all that exists were but a fermenting turmoil convulsed by obscure passions, what else would life be but despair?

The best way to install a ceiling fan is to hire an electrician. But if it's poetry you want, then you've got to find what you love.

Consciousness comes into existence when it is conscious of something, and conscious of being conscious of something. Make an incision, then remove the lyric: look at it wriggle, full of anxious life, unconscious life, a placenta swarming with words and avidity.

Can anything more closely resemble the lineaments of gestation than a sphagnum frog?

Language is simultaneously interior and exterior, like these lawn chairs. The tension between faith and reason is redeemed by absurdity. Grill accessories, patio umbrellas, resin sheds.

There are apparatuses, and then there are apparatuses. The world is alive with transcendence. Swans are signs of semantic absorption. Our interactions with the invisible forces of our lives can be partly achieved by fulfilling that wish to be drunk by one's own body, to become the pulp of a nourishing nullification and carouse into existence like a carnival. The history of a life, no matter what it may be, is a history of frustration. You can use that to your benefit. The coefficient of adversity engorges the physical with divine extension.

Drukpa Kunley's erection so stupefied a demon that he was able to slay it with a single blow.

The wheel recalls its circularity by rolling. The novel is avid to expand its scope and so becomes a fez. I am not here, thinks Kierkegaard, so much to exalt tools, as to use them. But how does one reconcile reason to the divine? How does a big-box retailer create a consistent merchandising voice?

"The pagan was gripped by anxiety when great fortune came his way, for he had a certain distrust of the gods. But in Christianity! One craves and strains after earthly goods, and then, to free oneself of that anxiety, thanks God!"[1] That is just how such Christendom becomes more worldly even than paganism.

The first stage to wealth is to become a sociopath.

But that's not how Christianity was meant work. It was not guaranteed by the manufacturer, and its relation to the temporal individual does not fit neatly into conceptual frameworks, and the outlet box and its support must be able to able to fully support the weight of the moving fan. The eternal is paradoxical because you cannot insert God in time.

1. From papers of Soren Kierkegaard.

The rejection of the actual and the projection of the possible is crucial. But don't reject everything without first sampling a little of what life has to offer in the way of webbing and paste. Being free means determining what one wants, not getting what one wants. These are the structural aspects of any given situation.

Making the electrical connections will be a little different. It is possible to solder aluminum but it is not easy. You can make crimp connections, but the contact resistance will be different than for a soldered piece of copper.

The divine is always present, we just don't see it. Don't let that discourage you.

Being is everywhere and offers a multitude of flavors, from cherries jubilee to the nutty coconut of perpetual possibility. We must question the meaning of being in order to be conscious of being conscious, which is like imprinting a sunset on a leather belt. You will have the impression but not the colors. You will have the general idea but not the breath and smell of it. I can identify almost any emotion by its weight. Though if it suddenly grows dark outside when I open a drawer of old letters, I cannot tell you why "salon" is such a pretty word. You might try selling wedding dresses on the side, or study granite. I am trying to fulfill my promise to the fjord. I have an iron emotion that obtrudes from my tongue. It's been a hard and diffcult winter and now I'm in the market for some patio furniture. I like to go for walks in the morning. This is when the divine is most apt to be trembling with vinegar. I carry an umbrella as if it were a universe of thread and little thin ribs. The weight of it proves the existence of rain. The sound of rain is charmed and delicate and charged with life. I'm not calling any more lawyers in North Dakota about mineral rights. I'm done with that. All I want now is to nail my worries down to a plank of indifference, and head toward that mountain in the breath of the morning.

Commentary

Prose is exposition. Poetry is disposition. Prose explains. Poetry floats. Fuse the two together and you have the complex tones of a bowed violin string, integer multiples of the fundamental frequency, or the sentence you started that suddenly turned celestial. Goofy. Aberrant. Strange.

Prose elucidates, tells people how to do drywall repair or adjust a camera setting. Poetry, as Keats so wonderfully describes it to the eager Abbie Cornish, playing Fanny Brawne in Jane Campion's brilliant movie *Bright Star,* is swimming. "A poem needs understanding through the senses. The point of diving in a lake is not immediately to swim to the shore; it's to be in the lake, to luxuriate in the sensation of water. You do not work the lake out. It is an experience beyond thought. Poetry soothes and emboldens the soul to accept mystery."

Prose and poetry are often separate impulses, but sometimes that creative urge to mess with language is a rainbow of propellants.

In his prose poem "The Thyrsus," Charles Baudelaire describes the central object as "a stick, a simple stick, a staff to hold up hops, a prop for training vines, straight, hard and dry." That's prose. Prose is the support, the framework for explanation. For diatribe. For elucidation. For structuring thought. But "around this stick in capricious convolutions, stems and flowers play and gambol, some sinuous and wayward, others hanging like bells, or like goblets up-side-down. And an amazing resplendence surges from this complexity of lines and of delicate or brilliant colors."

That's where the poetry comes in: it wraps its arabesques around the stick and creates a prodigy of convolution, convulsive swirls of liberated word and image.

Life itself may have emerged from a condition of intense disquiet. One might imagine a goopy amalgam of desire and obstacle bubbling and spurting its way into a chain of polymers hat begins—weirdly, spasmodically, ecstatically—to assume agency and movement. It evolves.

It elaborates. It tests and probes and tumbles and feels. It does cartwheels. It circulates. It generates more and more protein, cells, alertness. It becomes a cat: lightning with fur on it.

A snake oscillating through grass. A delirium dressed in seesaws.

It starts as a word and becomes a sentence which becomes an urgency which becomes a surge of meandering thought and idea, a dry hard stick enveloped in delicate brilliant colors.

In "Kierkegaard at Home Depot" I was able to mix a number of my obsessions and ambitions into a single piece of writing: grommets and God, paganism and Proust, Christian theology and hardware. I have a strong philosophical bent and wanted to get that in there, too. What is consciousness? What is language? What kind of tools do you need for some electrical work?

I want to explain things but I also want to have fun. I want to dive into the language and go to the bottom of the lake and see what's down there and come back up and describe what I've just seen to anyone willing to listen. I want the all-enveloping sensation of water, and to be able to communicate those sensations, sometimes in the lucidity of prose, sometimes in a delirium of verbal opacity. And sometimes the lake isn't a lake or a metaphor it's a gigantic hardware store.

Dzvinia Orlowsky

Vegreville Egg

Like a hornet caught in a jar, static buzzing between words, he yells from across Manitoba's endless ice into the phone, two provinces away from the world's second largest *pysanka,* a Ukrainian-style Easter egg. Black and gold tiled, it turns in the wind like a colossal weathervane. Holding two separate rotary phone extensions, my parents yell *It's Uncle Bohdan!* interrupting each other in excited disbelief. Squatted on the floor next to my mother's legs, I dress my naked Mary Poppins doll in spiked heels and pretend to also be happy. Mathematically mastered, steel-girdled, three and a half stories high, weighing in at 2.5 tons—*we simply had to see it*—a pleasant 1,181-mile drive from Ohio to Egg. We pack a picnic, boiled eggs and sardines. What did we know about roadside burgers? But more pressingly, what did we know of art? Except that our home—family and guests insisted—aside from not having a framed print of the egg—was filled with it: paintings by *our own kind* that *one day* my parents whispered to us as if revealing an important family secret would be *worth a fortune*—despite the fact that, it turns out, these were not master oil paintings but rather, acrylic cartoons of our people doing our-people kind of things—playing *Kitchkari,* Ukrainian ring toss, or dancing in red leather boots, multi-colored satin ribbons streaming from flower wreaths in women's hair, men sporting handle-bar mustaches—paintings that showed happy people, stomping and spinning in place.

Commentary

The publication of Stephen Berg's prose poetry collection, *Shaving,* in 1998 by Four Way Books provided a one-of-a-kind opportunity for me.

At that time, I was in my fifth year as a founding editor, and we had the good fortune of having Berg approach us about publishing his book. Back then, some writers still preferred to type their manuscripts, and Berg, being one of those writers, was not able provide us with a floppy disk. A fast typist, I volunteered to key it in for him—51 prose poems, 107 pages.

I'd published my first prose poem in 1973, but had pretty much abandoned the form thereafter in favor of verse. The immersion in Berg's book, getting to know it on a physical level by keying it in, re-ignited a deeper understanding and appreciation for what a prose poem can do. What I took from it, primarily, was how when compressed, different layers of thought and speculation can shape a reflective narrative into a lyrical piece that stretches from margin to margin.

With this consideration in mind, I began writing a sequence of prose poems about 10 years ago including "Vegreville Egg." This poem was written about a particular phone conversation recalled from childhood—a few shared moments of much excitement between my parents and a close immigrant friend discussing colossal national treasures, sure-fire investments, and "best kept secrets" of contemporary Ukrainian art. Characteristically, Ukrainians love to out yell or to interrupt each other in conversation. Maybe it's enthusiasm rather than rudeness, an inherited sense of rushing to say what you have to say before the other proverbial shoe drops and pulverizes your cultural nest egg or your mother tongue is altogether obliterated.

I wrote this as a prose poem because prose poetry, line to line, moves with greater fluidity and because it loves secrets, half-truths, and the implausible—all taken into consideration as part of one conversation. Its meandering syntactical cadences encourage a voice to travel greater distances—to spin stories, colorful and zestful—beyond demarcations, without ever leaving its frame.

Robert Perchan

Neandertal Hotline

Their tools were cruder than those of their *Homo sapiens* contemporaries, our ancestors. And there is evidence they could neither speak, except possibly in some proto-language devoid of nuances, sing, nor sign. They couldn't paint and apparently never tried. They were bulky and had heads with all the bone in front, an aesthetic mistake. Few of their remains show signs of no physical strife. They buried their dead. Which was a blessing, for now we better understand them. Their Afterlives.

If you would like to talk to one, dial the number printed on the back of this brochure. You will be able to see her on the screen, but she will not be able to see you. Not with those vacant eye sockets. Keep in mind that with this species sexual dimorphism was not pronounced and we are not always able to guarantee with absolute certainty whether the pelvic bones are those of a female or a male. You will have to take your chances.

They lived a long time ago and we wiped them out, we think. Nevertheless, it is possible some of them interbred with our ancestors. If, for any reason, you suspect that your physical appearance or your manual dexterity or your capacity to carry a tune is not, in any way, up to snuff, don't hesitate to call. We all know at least one person who simply cannot excel. You may be on the road to extinction and not even realize it. If you can get this through your thick skull, call now. And remember, you can say anything you like, and she won't be able to talk back. Complete anonymity is assured. She is waiting for you.

Commentary

Who were they really? Well, it appears they buried their dead. Made stone tools. Had brains as big as ours. Still, a race of true Others. Not in any existential philosophical sense, but in barebone fact. You could write a novel about a relic population and make them born killers or the world's original Flower Children. Who knows? You could connect them with our fabled Yetis and Sasquatches. Who dare gainsay you? I'm sure there will be a movie, if there hasn't already been. Special effects will be up to it, if the scriptwriters will not. None of this will satisfy the healthy imagination, beyond the momentary thrill of fanciful speculation.

Intellectually, they are an itch that begs to be scratched and then forgotten. An area of specialization for people called paleoanthropologists. Poetically, they are pretty much zip. Zilch. Unless you go in for Really Lost Causes. You could portray them as our bumbling incompetent brother or sister or distant cousin selves, as I suppose was the best I could do.

Insofar as they were like us, they are boring. Insofar as they were truly different, they are unfathomable. What a gulf! And yet is this not the story of so many of our prose poems—the propinquity of the humdrum and the miraculous. The way they nag at each other, like a husband and wife.

But I'm supposed to be commenting on a single prose poem here, not an entire species.

I wrote "Neandertal Hotline" (I'm spelling it in the scientific rather than the popular fashion, to give the whole business an air of rigor) after reading some books about old bones. Most of the time the books were not difficult. They were aimed at the general reader, i.e. you or me who really should be doing something else, like making sure Darwinian Evolution doesn't suddenly turn around and decide to rub us out.

But more than anything else, I envied the authors of these books. They were smart and confident and articulate and positively exuberant in their interpretation of the significance of the tiniest fragment of a molar. They were *driven* in the best sense of the word. They had *passion. Gusto.* And they weren't babbling on about art or literature or God, either. They were talking about an idea so cruel that the heart recoils from its implications—in spite of a century and a half of familiarity with it. Natural Selection. The Universe's dirtiest joke. The most profound inspiration in the annals of the human race.

Nothing new there. But suddenly I wanted to pack up and hop a flight and reinvent myself as a fossil hunter and commune with these superior beings at international conferences and in the field. Or, alternatively, chuck everything and blow my entire meager wad in the bars and stews of some Southeast Asian port city—and in line with the Law spread a good bit of my DNA around to boot. Anything but sit at home and knock out a darkly sardonic prose poem and wait for an end that will come. Unselected, again.

Jane Lunin Perel

Red Radio Heart

Carnelia is tired of her heart. It's too heavy. When she tries to sleep it bumps, then races. She pictures it, disentangling itself from the system that feeds it, then shrinking, escaping out of her mouth, rolling down the street. Sticky candy apple heart. Road kill heart. She could have a pig's heart. Or a red radio heart that would play jazz for her but not Bartok. Her heart in a yellow basket that Ella Fitzgerald has lost. Maybe Frankenstein will stagger out from behind the billboard that supports the war. He'll need a new heart, too. Maybe he'll scoop up hers and she'll be free of her clumsy overripe blood-orange heart. Meanwhile, the generals beef up attacks.

Commentary

The woman "Carnelia" who possesses the "Red Radio Heart" is telling the story of her "overripe … heart." It is a poem of aging and alienation, which I now realize connects to the ancient and still powerful notions and dogmas concerning what Barbara Creed has called the "Monstrous-Feminine," depicted so precisely by the writer of Leviticus 15:28-33. That passage reads: "When the woman's bleeding stops, she must count off seven days. Then she will be ceremonially clean. On the eighth day she must bring two turtledoves or two young pigeons and present them to the priest at the entrance of the Tabernacle. The priest will offer one for a sin offering and the other for a burnt offering. Through this process, the priest will purify her before the LORD for the ceremonial impurity caused by her bleeding.… These are the instructions for dealing with anyone who has a bodily discharge.…"

This language frames the great horror of defilement and shame Carnelia has of her female body and its impurities and that I shared as a teenager. But these ideas only created a maddening sense of injustice in me, although the shame resurfaced at times. So here in stating she is "tired of her heart," she is also "tired" of her body entirely, as it has been degraded by cultural and religious influences and experiencing the "discharges" of surgery.

In contrast now, Carnelia has a freedom to muse about what might happen to her heart when it "escapes out of her mouth" and transforms instantly into "Sticky candy apple heart. Road kill heart." Or it could be transformed into a "pig's heart." These metaphors are ironic, sardonic, and in their way they celebrate the marvelous transformation which takes place in prose poetry in which the poet is liberated from old shame and digs into the unconscious to find far flung images of escape. Granted stickiness and a death by out of bodiness are messy, but the heart has at last escaped.

In defining prose poetry, Michael Benedict asks "What are the special properties of the prose poem?" to which he answers with the words of Baudelaire, "a necessity to attend to the prickings of consciousness beyond ordinary formal requirements...." For me, prose poetry has liberated my capacity to speak directly from the unconscious. I revere this power and marvel that nothing we experience leaves us or disappears. The unconscious contains everything a poet must access through imagery. Memory is enlarged in the unconscious. "A yellow basket that Ella Fitzgerald has lost" reflects the great joy of memory that I have of listening to her singing that song with my father; he was not concerned with my spillage or bodily "discharge," but rather with my brain and my spirit.

Joy is laced through fatigue, and for me jokes go a long way in accepting surgical procedures and their overflowing margins. The "pig's heart" is a memory of a friend who had a heart valve replaced by a pig valve. When I called him to see how he was, he answered "oink, oink." Next in connection with transformation gone beyond what is terrifying, comes "Frankenstein will stagger out from behind the billboard that supports the war." Let us recall the discharge involved in his creation and in his distorted heart. Also, "the generals beefing up attacks" previews spillage on a massive scale.

In writing prose poems my metaphors have become enormous, macabre, but funny and ironic. I believe I am dictating images that derive directly from my unconscious. My writing reflects abjection and its opposite, joy and freedom. The wonders of prose poetry thrill my mind and spirit, while the rest of me sheds its original parts and secretions.

Mary Ruefle

Please Read

Once upon a time there was a bird, my God.
—Clarice Lispector

I am the yellow finch that came to her feeder an hour before she died. I was the last living thing she saw, so my responsibility was great. Yet all I did was eat. Through eight long months of winter the black oiled sunflower seeds had gone untouched—not a single one of my kind or any other kind had approached them. It was too much work. Even if we'd had the strength—which we did not, half-starved as we were—we were not in the mood to crack anything. On the morning of the twenty-second of April she took them away and refilled the feeding tube with sunflower heart—sheeny niblets whose hard outer husk had been stripped away by some faraway, intricate machine. She went back inside and waited. From my branch I could see her do the things she liked to do—she picked up a towel from off the floor, she filled out a card stopping the mail, she boiled water, she stared into space. She saw me coming. Her face flickered with, if not exactly joy, the ordinary wellspring of life. It's true there was a sheet of glass between us. But I could see the seeds of her eyes and the upturned corners of her mouth. I ate a heart. I turned my head. She looked at me as if I were the last living thing on earth. And as I was, I kept on eating.

Commentary

As this piece was written some time ago I can't be sure, but I probably wrote it on April 22nd, and slipped the date in. I have no problem with anthropomorphism, none at all; I love writing in the supposed voice of inanimate objects or animals who don't speak English. Here I speak in the voice of a bird. Doubtless I was sitting in my apartment and doing nothing, feeling ill and dowdy, probably in my bathrobe, and watching the bird feeder through a set of double glass doors and wondering what it would be like to reverse the bird-watching to people-watching. The woman in the piece is dying, and there's a kind of linguistic haze that conflates things, that brings in images of a hospital (feeding tubes, machines, the sheet of glass) and also the sense that the living have no choice but to go on living, go on eating, we all do that, we sneak off to the hospital snack bar and eat … all the while the world is stopping for the dying, they aren't eating.

But everything I've said is, hopefully, in the piece itself. As it is based on direct observation, most of what can be said about it is obvious. Observation is like that. As a writer I like to observe things as much as I like to invent them.

Maureen Seaton

Fisher

I understood that in the time it took him to tie one mayfly I could open the fridge and remove the rainbow he caught the week before, fire up the grill, cook the fish, and eat it alone on our deck, with thyme and butter.

That when the fly was finished, uncannily real, freakishly swattable, another needed tying because the concentration it took was so lovely (and the mayflies themselves so elegant) the task demanded repeating.

I understood that his silhouette bent over light was precious, and the resolve he needed to wade the current, flick the wrist, flick it again until I dreamt of him up to his thighs in river, was formidable and ripe with faith.

And I understood that the man I loved thrived deep inside the fisher man in the swirling cold, the tidal stream, and for one moment away from the world and its demons, I could almost touch him.

Still, I left the quiet of his dying, where he glowed bright with purpose, and drove madly alone down the Hudson before he had a chance to bait his hook with mayflies, tree frogs, bloodsuckers.

Commentary

If memory serves me (good luck with that one!), the first time I heard a poet read a poem in prose was at the library in Tarrytown, NY, late eighties. I'd been writing for a few years—mostly 10-syllable lines that flowed in and out like waves (or punches)—and I was as open to surprise as a glowy new poet could be. I was also coming out of a divorce with kids, no job skills, a whole lot of confusion, curiosity, and WTF, and Alicia Ostriker got up and read "Cambodia."

Imagine that.

When I moved to Chicago in '91, I entered a world of poets that was acutely concerned with page or stage, theory or story, opaque or transparent, and on top of the list, language, upon which everyone seemed to agree. The poetry community was happily navigable, if contentious, and I found myself brave enough in the midst of the fray to break from the short line and type all the way to the side of the page. When I purchased my first computer in '94, the line kept rolling on until I started collaging my own chunks of text and all hell broke loose for me. I read at De Paul University one time and asked the audience if what I was reading sounded like poetry to them. Not only had I abandoned the line, but my work looked nothing like the prose poems I'd discovered and loved—Russell Edson's and Maxine Chernoff's. I called my work collage poems because I used cut and paste methods to organize the parts, but they were really long prose poems with lots of parataxis and apparent loose ends. They were narrative at heart, but nonlinear and with an edge.

The audience at De Paul said "Yes!" after I read my collaged prose poem about Amelia Earhart, and I was relieved.

Last week I met with a young poet from Colorado who is currently struggling with the prose poem herself. If she relinquishes the line, is she still a poet? (It's 2018, twenty-five years away from my own struggle.) And my undergrads balk as well. They think it's cheating. Do whatever you want, I tell them, you're poets! And I invite them to see *writing as infinite possibility.* (Alicia Ostriker).

I once wrote about the prose poem as a fast car, how the sound of the words arrived first, no interruptions, no restraints, the rhythm kicking in—my twin turbo six-cylinder cutting through wind—all horizon and velocity. That's still true much of the time. Other times I cut and paste and end up with a lyric essay. This time, writing "Fisher," I meditated on a relationship that called for a container with sturdy sides: a repository, a mine, a bomb. Holding the poem in my hand, I let it go.

Alicia Ostriker, "Cambodia," from *The Mother/Child Papers* (Momentum Press, 1980; Beacon Press, 1986; U of Pittsburgh Press, 2009)

"An Interview with Alicia Ostriker by Susan Rushing Adams," https://www.utdallas.edu/ah/reunion/interviews/ostriker/

David Shumate

End of the Year

We sit together to tally up our losses. The people who have died. The animals who have retreated to their better heavens. We discuss where we want to have our ashes scattered and who can sing at our funerals and who must keep their mouths shut. We make maps of the countries we travel to in our dreams and point out our favorite rivers. The orchards where the fruit is always public. The small towns where people drive trucks and speak to the dogs sitting at their side. We flip through the calendar on the table. It seems too small to record all that's gone on. You search for the day you accepted you were not immortal. I scan for the day my final virginity disappeared. You grab April with both hands and tear it down the middle. I take hold of November and yank. We throw the shreds of one month after another into a bucket. I light the first match and give a whoop. You light the next and whisper a prayer.

Commentary

"End of the Year" is an old man's poem, a poem gazing backwards rather than forward, a poem "taking stock of things," as we used to say. It is a poem about how we confront our own mortality, the fact that the clock is ticking. This poem skirts that thin frontier between the quietly tragic and the mildly comic. It leans heavily on common diction, common imagery. No pirouettes here. No pyrotechnics. No vanishing acts. It doesn't pull and strain at the reins of the English language. It moves forward at a gentle trot. And it doesn't want to call much attention to itself along the way. It is in search of the elemental, those enduring images that remain once all the glitter has dulled. It ends with the ceremonial burning of the symbols of the past.

On the surface, because it relinquishes the line break, it falls into the category of the prose poem, that little theater of the poetic world that pours its images and language out in a thin, uninterrupted stream. That five-act play squashed into a short scene. If anything remains for a reader after having set the poem down, I hope it is the faint scent of smoke rising from the page. And maybe a little heat.

Charles Simic

I was stolen by the gypsies. My parents stole me right back. Then the gypsies stole me again. This went on for some time. One minute I was in the caravan suckling the dark teat of my new mother, the next I sat at the long dining room table eating my breakfast with a silver spoon.

It was the first day of spring. One of my fathers was singing in the bathtub; the other one was painting a live sparrow the colors of a tropical bird.

Commentary

I remember the night well. It was quarter to three and I was about to compose a poem. My dog Igor was barking viciously at the moon out in the yard and getting on my nerves. In my laboratory, Ligeia had just put the final cleaning touches to a test tube and was reaching for a jar labeled *prose poetry* on the shelf, when to my horror I noticed that this admirable woman of rare learning known for her singular yet placid cast of beauty was chewing bubble gum. I threw a fit so loud and protracted, it even made that stupid dog out there shut up. You'd think, I asked heaven to be my witness, that after everything she had to put up cohabitating with that bum and souse, Edgar Poe, she'd have learned how to conduct herself in the presence of another lofty poetic genius sensitive to the slightest distraction? I must have blacked out after that, since I remember nothing else of that horrible night.

So how did the poem get written then? I've no idea. What I can swear on a stack of Bibles is that never in my life did I sit down with the intention of writing a prose poem. My book of untitled prose fragments, *The World Doesn't End,* was not originally labeled prose poetry. In fact, the manuscript I sent to the publishers wasn't called anything. What I had done is to copy some of my nearly illegible scribblings from old notebooks, which after I rediscovered them and read them, struck me as having poetic qualities of their own and strung all together surprisingly read like a tongue-in-cheek autobiography. After tinkering over them for several months and reducing the manuscript to sixty-eight pieces, I showed them to my editor at Harcourt who to my surprise offered to publish them. However, just before the book was to appear, I got an urgent call from her asking me what do we call this? Don't call it anything, I told her, but she explained to me that a book needs to be called something, so that libraries and bookstores know on what shelf to put it. After giving the matter some thought, I agreed to call it prose poetry.

Looking at the poem today, I can guess what was in my mind when I wrote it. Warning children about being stolen by the gypsies if they wander off is a stock phrase East European grandmothers and mothers use to scare children. As a city kid, stuck living in an apartment building, the life of the gypsies, from what I saw of it in Yugoslavia, seemed far more attractive to me. Of course, I knew my little tale about how I kept changing identities had to be short. I had read and liked plenty of prose poetry before I wrote what I wrote here, but I admired most of all the brevity and stunning lunacy of Max Jacob's, Daniil Kharms' and Russell Edson's finest poems. They are like parlor magic tricks which make you scratch your head after you see them, like the one called "Miser's Dream" where a seemingly infinite supply of coins is plucked out of the air by the magician. That's the marvel of a prose poem too. It looks like prose on the page, but acts like a poem in your head.

Thomas R. Smith

Brushpile Sparrows

It's good to have a brushpile in your back yard. Accumulation of last year's storm-fall, it's a waist-high sheaf or wave, shapely as if composed. In mid-winter, a dozen sparrows make it their home, or if not their home, their base. In daylight one may see them clumped like thickenings of the top branches, dark beads along the curving roof beams of their stick-house. Within the snow-thatched tangle, shelter from wind and predators, shadowy flittings … I leave crumbs and seeds for them on a round concrete slab earmarked for a future garden project, the powder snow on top of it printed by delicate claws. Some say that God got the idea for human beings by observing birds' flight. When I approach, twelve sparrows flutter up into the black walnut tree. They make a kind of visual music, like fingers lightly brushing the strings of a harp. Watching and listening, I feel as though I'm seeing my own soul. Come spring, I'll clear it away, knowing the rain and wind will keep doing their work, and I'll begin to gather up another pile.

Commentary

At a significantly earlier point in our thirty-two-year-and-counting marriage, my wife Krista and I drove to a nearby state park to take part in a summer morning's "bird walk." We were not then and are not now birders. Almost everyone else on the bird identification walk along the Willow River was older than us, and it all felt uncomfortably *senior citizen* to me at the time. What point in these fine distinctions between warblers? On our way home I remarked intemperately, "If I end up that way, please shoot me!" I must have thought my elderly hiking companions' time would be better spent writing poems!

The joke that life subsequently played on me was that, not so many years later, I came to find unexpected solace in the companionship of wild birds during the George W. Bush reign of error. Suddenly, with the right wing ruling by fear and perpetrating a ruinous oil war in the Mideast, I noticed that I newly recognized and very much needed the comforting presence of those winged nonhuman "others" who do not share our capacity for mechanized mass slaughter. It wasn't so much a new affection as the heightened consciousness of an old one (I had, after all, originally consented with some anticipation to the bird walk). Suddenly, as never before, I was writing bird poems. In a year of springtime bombing, the appearance of the first robin became an emotionally overwhelming emblem of what was still right with the world. Birds, like much else in life, repay in direct proportion the attention we give them. And in our accelerating environmental crisis, it's once again all too easy to imagine the loneliness and silence of a world without birdsong, against which Rachel Carson prophetically warned us.

Bird enthusiasts say that one of the best and simplest things a homeowner can do for resident birds is to allow or even cultivate a patch of wildness in one's yard where they (and other small creatures) may shelter. In Wisconsin where I live this means most crucially protection from brutal onslaughts of the northern winter. As described in the poem, I annually violate neighborhood standards of yard upkeep by piling windfalls into what, by winter, has become a stickly yurt or wigwam of interwoven branches, dark and still at its heart, a safe place out of the wind and snow. And for more than one crushing cold snap, gangs of sparrows have adopted it as their base, while never becoming tame enough not to react to my nearness with their exquisitely musical group ascent to the branches still attached to our towering black walnut.

The beautifully strange idea that God thought up human beings while observing the flight of birds I found in the philosopher Jacob Needleman's profound book *An Unknown World: Notes on the Meaning of the Earth.* Needleman himself discovered that little legend on the back of a postcard showing details of a sculpture above one of the porches of Chartres Cathedral in Paris. In what is essentially a poet's response, Needleman let himself be deeply thrilled in spite of the questionable provenance of this explanation of human origin, "offered by who knows what authority, and with who knows what evidence."

I relish letting some of the deliciously odd ideas I encounter in my reading enter my prose poems. One of the peculiar virtues of the prose poem lies, as Robert Bly has noted, in its capacity for absorbing detail that might fit less comfortably a more conventional lined poem. I've cherished and taken advantage of the prose poem's forgiving elasticity which indeed allows, even encourages the poet to pile on the details to his or her heart's content. I've noticed too that the very density of certain prose poems can formally echo their content in a uniquely satisfying way. (A brilliant example is Nin Andrews's "Red Blossoms," which seduces the reader's eye, along with the poem's pollen-gathering bee, into an intoxicating floral/print labyrinth.) Because I like to throw the windfalls of thought, feeling, intuition, and experience onto the sentence-pile of the prose poem, "Brushpile Sparrows" thus becomes an image of the prose poem medium itself.

Liz Waldner

Now How I Am an American

The wind carries cloud, highway racket and spruce needles, all around and above my head. There's water here, an island surround, and sun after days of cold rain. After a week's disdain, the cat lies at my feet, having another in her 12 years of baths. Not my cat, but courted, petted, called to and today, at last, brushed. For days she'd turned her back whenever I appeared, studying whatever was opposite me. Now opposite me, she licks her stripes. She's beautiful. The cloud's beautiful, incised in sky with a breeze's water motif. It's the same as a petroglyph crab. With nimbus.

Now gone. That quick. So, too, the quick part of the quick and the dead, really. Fifty years feels the same as between this bee and me: in the second grade in my strange finery, the furry purple plaid pleated skirt and matching vest that laced, always too big, crunching acorns on the way to sing with my classmates the Thanksgiving hymn in a church: *Sing praises to his name he forgets not his own.* I could remember my name; why could I not be praised? I wanted praise, or so I thought. What I meant was to be invisible, by which I meant perfect. Only perfection would not be hurt. The time I led my fellow Brownies into the wrong car in the parking lot. Bellowing, beating, humiliation; contempt and its shadow, shame, abounding. Indeed, knowing is not enough; the years, as zeroes, adding up. To nothing, I mean.

They drive fast here. This time here is British Columbia where British Columbia is Vancouver Island. Not fast but far faster than the speed limit; it is noted with disdain that the Albertans do not. Here costs in kilograms and liters. Said KILL o meter not ki LOM uh ter. And manifests either a familiar redneck outrage at foreigner or a generous good cheer, each underlain by understanding that the US (which, yes yes, thinks it is America) thinks Canada is its colony, loot, loon, raw material. A gentler disdain and pity for us dispensed by the educated: *how could you know? There is nothing in your newspapers at all....*

Here the sweat bee replaced by yellow jacket: my presence usually means lunch. The cat's had a bit by now and comes, tail up, to be petted, then brushed. Says her cat sound. Sound of soughing cedars now. Now not. Cloud, nimbus, of cat hair, and not. I have my diagnosis; I begin to colonize the not.

Commentary

A peculiarly "American" tendency: to think of one's life-story, circumstance, or history as entirely one's own creation.

If you're a "winner," congrats, it's all down to you. If not, it's your fault, entirely your most private, personal, shameful fault. You have failed to "live your life to the fullest/follow your bliss;" caused yr cancer/prevented the prosperity that God wants for you; failed to propitiate your ancestors ($2k for Family Constellation Therapy); have really bad luck/suck at life/are WRONG in your being; knew better than to ____ while ____ (rapey rapey); didn't think/choose/get born/act right: be gone.

In other words, *it's your misfortune and none of my own,* little dogie. Not structures/strictures inherent in a capitalist, misogynist, racist, brutal, may all beings be dead sort of enterprise. The land of the individual everything where, if you got a problem the problem is you, so better you don't know nothing. Opioid crisis? Duh. Let the unhoused/unfed first work 20 hours a week. So, you're in Ben Carson's crosshairs (another horrible Romper Room-like mirror), asked to believe what happens around/to kids (bang bang) has nothing to do with how their lives turn out.

Er, I digress. This poem is interested in how to know what you do and don't know, has takes on time, takes time with time, lets causes and effects propose themselves to others and ease, if sadden, with memory and beauty. It refers to previous poems, especially those (aha) in *Saving the Appearances:* memory, identity and the uses of things....

We live in multiple little and big houses, even when homeless: language is half in us and half in those worlds around us; our experience comprises/inflected by hearts, minds, bodies, actions, laws, events we call our own and/or others'. Thoughts, words, selves as prisons and freedoms. My life nested in every other; trace a way with words into/ among others—and be-with.

Prose poems let there be that connective life, eh? (as those Canadians or at least Quebecois say). It's just one thing after another. And then it isn't.

Rosmarie Waldrop

From *Lawn of Excluded Middle*

I worried about the gap between expression and intent, afraid the world might see a fluorescent advertisement where I meant to show a face. Sincerity is no help once we admit to the lies we tell on nocturnal occasions, even in the solitude of our own heart, wishcraft slanting the naked figure from need to seduce to fear of possession. Far better to cultivate the gap itself with its high grass for privacy and reference gone astray. Never mind that it is not philosophy, but raw electrons jumping from orbit to orbit to ready the pit for the orchestra, scrap meanings amplifying the succession of green perspectives, moist fissures, spasms on the lips.

Commentary

The prose poem is well over a hundred years old and has been practiced by such illustrious poets as Baudelaire and Rimbaud, but it still causes puzzlement. In the GDR before the Iron Curtain came down, Elke Erb told me, it was not accepted as a literary form at all.

It is both an attraction and the problematic of the prose poem that it is a step farther removed from the oral than verse, that its effects, its rhythms are subtler, less immediate. That if it counts, it counts words or sentences rather than stresses or syllables.

Yet, the prose poem is not a short-short-short story. Of the two terms yoked together in its name *poem* is the more important. It needs to have the poem's density and intensity. It must take wing.

Why do I write prose poems? I sometimes wonder, because I like verse very much: the way its rhythm rises from the tension between line and sentence; the way it refuses to fill up all of the available space of the page, each line acknowledging what is *not.* It makes manifest that "to create is to make a pact with nothingness" (Clark Coolidge). Or, as Heather McHugh put it: "[poetry] is the very art of turnings, toward the white frame of the page, toward the unsung, toward the vacancy made visible, that wordlessness in which our words are couched."

So for me one great challenge of the form is to compensate for its absence of turning, or margin. I try to place the vacancy *inside* the text. I cultivate cuts, discontinuity, leaps, shifts of reference. "Gap gardening," I have called it, and my main tool for it is collage.

But the excitement is that the prose poem, even more than a poem in verse, each time sets out into uncharted territory:

"Moving on in the Dark like Loaded Boats at Night, though there is no Course, there is Boundlessness" (Emily Dickinson).

Charles Harper Webb

Handsome Can Sit Up by Himself,

Erik declares, holding Grandma's gift: a plush new teddy bear.

"Fev can do that," answers Dad, who bought Fev the day Erik was born.

Fev's fur is coarser than Handsome's. He has stump-legs and, lying on his back—all he's really built to do—looks more like a hairy gingerbread man than a bear.

"Fev's legs don't bend," Erik says. "He can't sit up."

"Neither can Hamstrung," counters Dad.

"Yes he can!" Erik sits Handsome on his bed. "His name's Handsome."

Handsome sits well, it's true. His ample rear is made for it. His back legs bend just right. His well-formed front feet, spread to offer bear-hugs, add stability. Until Dad shoves him down.

"Fev sits better than that," Dad says. (His wife calls Fev "that sad old thing.")

"You knocked him down," Erik protests.

"No I didn't. Poor Hamster lost his balance," Dad says.

"His name's Handsome," Erik says, and sits the bear back up. He's watched *Monty Python* with Dad, but doesn't grasp, at 4, the finer points of Silliness. Still, Dad shoves Handsome down again, then blatantly hides his own hands.

"You pushed him," Erik explains. "Tell the truth!"

That stops Dad cold. Instead of God, their family venerates Truth.

"I might've bumped him," Dad admits. He slept with *his* Fev every night, rubbing him against his nose until there was a slick, shiny, bare *nose-place* on Fev's face.

Erik's Fev has the start of a nose-place.

When Erik sets Handsome down out of Dad's reach, Dad says, "Hambone may not be sitting on his own. Maybe it's magic."

"Tell the truth!" Erik demands, then reminds, "His name's Handsome."

"Sometimes it's hard to know what's true," Dad says.

"There's no such thing as magic," Erik states. "Ms Nune said."

Ms Nune is his pre-school teacher: a Russian-Armenian with, Dad can see, a classically materialist point of view.

The truth is, Handsome *is* handsome: a Kodiak, most likely, his fur thick, brown and sleek as if he's spent weeks yanking salmon from clear, rushing streams, stuffing his handsome face with them, as well as wild berries and honey, then washing in the river's cold gush, letting the sun dry him as it burns down on the glorious Arctic summer that's finished almost before it's begun.

Commentary

When my son was very young, we started playing what I thought of as absurdist games. Lord knows what he thought of them. In any case, he soon got the hang, and seized on his role as Voice of Reason when I'd say, for instance, "My real name is Bomba Fudge." (Yes, I've written about that, too.) One of us coined the term "dobba-dobba" to describe a person who makes an idiotic claim—"If you don't go to my church, you're going to hell"—and can't be reasoned out of it. *Arguing with a dobba-dobba* became our term for futility (and the title of another poem). In my role as Dad, I often took—sometimes intentionally, sometimes not—the dobba-dobba role.

Our games provided lots of laughs, and not, I hope, too much befuddlement for my son. I liked to think I was preparing him for the world: both the frustration of talking to idiots, and the fun of letting his mind go really strange.

I often do the latter in my poems—especially prose poems, which seem the natural habitat of the strange. I don't consider theme or even "meaning" when I write a poem. I try to set down words and images that, preferably for unknown reasons, interest me. Once the thing is done, I consider if, and how, it might interest others, too.

Now that "Handsome" has been written, certain themes are clear. One is that Dad believes his childhood was the way childhoods should be. That's why he buys the kind of cheap, old-fashioned bear he himself owned, and goes so far as to impose the name he gave his own bear: *Fev.*

When Fev is supplanted by a more expensive, modern, better-made bear, Dad resists. He mocks the new bear's good looks and boastful name. In the guise of play, he tries to humble the new bear. Enjoined to "tell the truth," he equivocates with talk of magic and uncertainty. Yet even this escape from facticity is thwarted by a Higher Authority: the pre-school teacher, Ms Nune.

What happens next in the poem came to me as one of those surprises that make writing poems so much fun. The fact that the surprise still moves me today suggests that it came straight from my Unconscious, where all the good stuff hides.

Dad starts by doing what no true dobba-dobba ever does: he admits that he was wrong. Handsome deserves his name. He's a good teddy bear—handsome enough to be a real bear, fresh from an Edenic Arctic summer.

Like that summer, Erik's childhood will be "finished almost before it's begun." But how glorious, Dad hopes, that brief run will be.

Tom Whalen

The Doll Writes to Her Mother

1

The way you are neglecting me is mystifying. Nevertheless (I almost wrote *nerve*theless) here's what I've learned: a house, a table, a finger. She tells me I am not to be released because I am mad. Well, I don't tell her my mother made me so. The house is strange. At night I am not alone in it. Her parents sleep on shelves. I want to study astronomy, but I'm afraid you won't approve. Where are you? For hours she stares at me without saying anything. Please write.

2

Mother, she is baking bread made of locomotives. She wants me to starve my sisters. She doesn't sing me to sleep like you used to do. I have no money, no clothes. Are you, Mother, naked in the eyes of your maker? I'm listening to the watches in the shoe box. They want to tell me something. They want not to be watches, but watchmen who turn the night into day. At night she does not cover me. She sits on the sill in the nightdress that used to belong to you. At one breast she holds a frog, at the other a dung beetle. Midnight.

Commentary

One morning I began a series of prose poems about dolls. No question or hesitation for me at all that the prose poem would be my form of choice into these otherworldly creatures upon whom we exercise our imaginations and who both attract and repel, as only they should. Did we dream them into being or they us? I tried to imagine their consciousness, their physicality, their metaphysics and fears. What would doll ontology be? How might it resemble ours, how differ?

In "A Doll Writes to Her Mother," as in many of the poems in the series, the differences are both less than one might expect and more. The doll is mystified that her mother is not there for her. She fears the child (?) by whom she is now kept. How strange this new world is for the doll. Why do her new keeper's parents sleep, doll-like, on shelves? And why does the doll want to study astronomy, and why does she fear this won't meet her mother's approval? And why is her keeper dressed in her mother's old nightgown and the doll left uncovered at night? So much the doll and we don't understand about the doll's new home.

Other dolls in the series, less troubled, possess a porcelain clarity regarding their ontology. In "Romanticism and Dolls," for example, dolls at night "imagine they can capture, in glass jars, light off wet leaves. But they know they can't, not really. Not everything can be real, they know, or red or flowing."

If poetry, as Breton wrote, is the saddest road that leads to everything, then who better than the saddest of the inanimates, with whom we're so intimately entwined, to accompany us there?

Peter Wortsman

The Back of Words

We only ever get to see the back of words, the hardened husk in the rot of talkative entrails, only the dried blood of impact—poor flattened insect—alpine blossom drained of its perfume. We only smell the odor of dead words, of mute mummies, cadaverous hieroglyphs. Even the traces never stop telling.

Commentary

A word about the poem itself. Though language is my tool and toy of choice, and I keep teasing out its possibilities, I feel perennially frustrated by its innate limitations, its reticence to reveal more than the surface, its stubborn reluctance to do more than describe. As to the method of composition, I sometimes play tricks with myself, spinning the initial silken thread of a text in another tongue out of the cocoon of the unconscious to confound and tease the ego in what amounts to a kind of mirror writing, and then, to shift metaphors, tug at the line, bringing back my catch in English. In this case the original was fished in French, my third language. (See below.) The twice-born text ought rightfully to appear in a bilingual format. The creative process works as an extreme constraint paradoxically freeing up a string of associations, true to Rimbaud's premise, *Je est un autre* (I is another)—especially in a second tongue. As the bilingual reader will notice, the English is not a translation per se, but rather a loose adaptation produced with considerable poetic license:

Le dos des mots

On ne cueille jamais que le dos des mots, la carapace qui subsiste après le pourissement des entrailles bavardes, que le sang sec après l'impact—pauvre insecte aplati—fleur alpine dépouillée de son parfum. On ne sent que l'odeur des mots morts, des momies muettes, cadavres de hiéroglyphes. Même les traces ne cessent jamais de raconter.

Gary Young

A Woman Leans

A woman leans against a tall white pine, looks up into the tree, then lowers her head and stares at the horizon. Her son has climbed into the branches high above her. She's called him down twice, but afraid now her voice might distract him, she stands there silently and waits for him to fall. She knows if he does, there is nothing she can do. A cold wind moves through the tree. She can feel her body stiffen, but does not look up when the child cries out, I can see almost forever.

Commentary
"Finding the Poem: Some Notes on Form"

I have been asked on more than one occasion to defend the prose poem, and to explain in particular how a poem can be a poem without "the line." Curiously, it is often poets working in free verse who make the most strenuous objection to prose poems, the same poets who argue for the legitimacy of free verse against those who champion poems written in formal meter and rhyme. Both arguments are absurd, and disingenuous as well. One might just as well be asked to defend the sonnet.

The prose poem has a history in the poetry of Europe and America that extends back more than a century and a half. It was appropriated by many of those same poets who first experimented with other free verse forms, and of course in China the *fu,* or poem-in-prose, has a history that stretches back millennia.

After Apollinaire's *Calligrams* and the visual explosions of Dada, after Modernism, Concrete poetry, Visual poetry, Language poetry and all the rest, to question the legitimacy of any poetic form is pedantic and unproductive. I am neither a critic, nor an apologist. I am simply a poet who has followed his appetites and his instincts to a congenial form.

My embrace of the prose poem is the result of a confluence in my work as a poet and my work as a fine printer. When I published *The Geography of Home,* an artists' book in which the text runs in a single horizontal line across each page, I found myself seduced by a form that literally embodied the semantic landscape I was attempting to inhabit. My use of the prose poem is not based on any philosophic projection; it is rather a matter of enthusiasm and practicality.

The paradox of any poetic form is that it simultaneously liberates and constricts. Any formal strategy will structure a specific logic, and every form accentuates or encourages a particular mode of thinking; I am tempted to say, a particular mode of wonder. Form is merely an architecture necessary to support the ceremony of the poem.

Readers come to every poem with certain expectations, and traditional poetic forms create an anticipation of the "poetic" that prose does not. It is this very lack of expectation that makes the prose poem supremely subversive and supple; the reader may be seduced in wholly unanticipated ways. By eschewing the ornamental apparatus of received poetic forms, the prose poem must rely wholly on the music and the honesty of its own utterance. When they're successful, prose poems achieve a subtlety and a power to convince seldom matched by lineated poems.

The reader's diminished expectation of a poetic experience also makes the prose poem an especially demanding form. There are no signposts that telegraph: this is a poem. Because it is prose, and shares more visual equivalence with the language we use to negotiate newspapers, contracts or personal correspondence, it must work especially hard to embrace the rapture of language we identify as poetry.

My attraction to the prose poem is emotional rather than critical. The prose poem is a maternal form. It is comforting and embracing, but it can also be smothering, constricting; once inside there is no way out, no place to rest until the poem is finished. It is a clot of language, and must convince through revelation.

But in truth, what I treasure most about this form is the moral pressure it exerts. The prose poem encourages a particular kind of modesty. It might even at times achieve a certain humility, a humility which may, through grace, be reflected back upon the poet's own heart.

Contributors' Biographies

Kim Addonizio is the author of a dozen books, most recently the poetry collection *Mortal Trash* (W. W. Norton, 2017) and a memoir-in-essays, *Bukowski in a Sundress: Confessions from a Writing Life* (Penguin, 2016).

Robert Alexander is the author, most recently, of *Richmond Burning,* a chapbook of prose poems from Red Dragonfly Press. He is the founding editor of the Marie Alexander Poetry Series at White Pine Press. robertalexander.info.

John Allman has published eight books of poetry, the first being *Walking Four Ways in the Wind,* which appeared in The Princeton Series of Contemporary Poets. He has just completed his ninth book, *Deep Breath: New & Selected Poems 2004–2017.*

Jack Anderson, a poet and dance writer, is the author of eleven books of poetry including, most recently, *Backyards of the Universe* (Hanging Loose Press, 2017), and *Traffic: New and Selected Prose Poems,* which won the Marie Alexander Award for Prose Poetry (White Pine Press, 1993). *His Ballet and Modern Dance: A Concise History* (Princeton Book Company, 1993) has entered its third edition.

Nin Andrews' poems have appeared in many literary journals and anthologies including *Ploughshares, Agni, The Paris Review,* and four editions of *Best American Poetry.* The author of seven chapbooks and seven full-length poetry collections, her most recent book, *Miss August,* was published by CavanKerry Press in 2017. ninandrews.com.

Sally Ashton, Editor-in-Chief of *DMQ Review,* is the author of three books. Her fourth, *The Behaviour of Clocks,* was released in 2019 from WordFarm.

Michael Benedikt's legendary anthology *The Prose Poem: An International Journal* was responsible for encouraging many of the poets in this anthology to write prose poems. His two most influential books of prose poems were *Night Cries* and *Mole Notes,* both published by Wesleyan University Press.

Robert Bly's prose poems were most recently collected in *Reaching Out to the World* (White Pine Press, 2009). His essays on fairy tales appear in *More Than True* (Henry Holt, 2018), and W. W. Norton brought out his *Collected Poems* in the fall of 2018.

A painter and print-maker, **Greg Boyd** is also the author of novels, collections of short stories, and illustrated books of prose poems.

John Bradley's prose poems can be found in *You Don't Know What You Don't Know* (CSU Poetry Center, 2010). His newest book, *Erotica Atomica* (WordTech Editions, 2017), offers both nuclear-related prose poems and verse.

Joel Brouwer is the author of four books of poems, including *Off Message* (Four Way Books, 2016). He is chair of the Department of English at The University of Alabama.

Mairéad Byrne emigrated from Ireland to the United States in 1994, for poetry. Her most recent poetry collections are *Famosa na sua cabeça* (Dobra Editorial, 2015), *You Have to Laugh* (Barrow Street, 2013), and *The Best of (What's Left of) Heaven* (Publishing Genius, 2010, reprinted 2019). Current publications include two chapbooks, *In & Out* (Smithereens, 2019) and *har sawlya* (above/ground, 2019). She lives in Providence and teaches at Rhode Island School of Design.

Maxine Chernoff is the author of sixteen books of poetry and six works of fiction. She has won an NEA, the PEN Translation Award, and has been a Visiting Writer at the American Academy in Rome

Laura Chester is the editor of many anthologies and has published volumes of poetry, prose and non-fiction, most recently *Rancho Weirdo* (Bootstrap Press, 2008), *Sparks* (The Figures, 2010), and *Riding Barranca* (Trafalgar Square Books, 2013). laurachester.com.

Kim Chinquee's most recent collection is *Wetsuit.* She's senior editor of *New World Writing,* chief editor of *Elm Leaves Journal,* and she co-directs the writing major at SUNY-Buffalo State.

Brian Clements is co-editor with Jamey Dunham of *An Introduction to the Prose Poem* (Firewheel Editions) and co-editor with Alexandra Teague and Dean Rader of *Bullets into Bells: Poets and Citizens Respond to Gun Violence* (Beacon Press, 2017). He founded and edited *Sentence: A Journal of Prose Poetics* and, among other collections, has several books of prose poems with Quale Press—most recently *A Book of Common Rituals,* 2014.

Peter Conners is author of nine books of poetry, fiction, and nonfiction. His prose-poetry collections include *Of Whiskey & Winter* and *The Crows Were Laughing in their Trees,* both from White Pine Press. He lives with his family in Rochester, NY, where he works as Publisher of BOA Editions, Ltd.

Jon Davis is the author of five chapbooks and six full-length poetry collections—*Dangerous Amusements, Scrimmage of Appetite, Preliminary*

Report, Heteronymy: An Anthology, Improbable Creatures, and An Amiable Reception for the Acrobat. His seventh full-length collection, *The Many-Body Problem,* is forthcoming from Grid Books.

Peter Davis' books of poems are *Hitler's Mustache, Poetry! Poetry! Poetry!, TINA,* and *Band Names and Other Poems.* More about his writing and music at artisnecessary.com.

A poet, critic and musician, **Michel Delville** has authored many books on literature and the arts, including *The American Prose Poem: Poetic Form and the Boundaries of Genre* (U. Florida Press, 2008). Two of his prose-poetry collection were translated into English by Gian Lombardo and published by Quale Press: *Third Body,* 2008; *Anything & Everything,* 2016. He teaches English and American literatures, as well as comparative literatures, at the University of Liège, where he directs the Interdisciplinary Center for Applied Poetics.

Chard deNiord is the poet laureate of Vermont and author of six books of poetry, most recently *Interstate* (U. Pittsburgh Press, 2015) and *The Double Truth* (U. Pittsburgh Press, 2011). He is also the author of a book of interviews with nine American poets (Galway Kinnell, Jane Hirshfield, Carolyn Forché, Martín Espada, Stephen Kuusisto, Ed Ochester, Peter Everwine, Stephen Sandy, Natasha Trethewey) and James Wright's widow, Anne Wright, titled *I Would Lie To You If I Could.* He is a professor of English and Creative Writing at Providence College, where he has taught since 1998, and trustee of the Ruth Stone Trust. He lives in Westminster West, VT, with his wife Liz.

Karen Donovan is the author of *Your Enzymes Are Calling the Ancients* (Persea Books, 2016) and *Fugitive Red* (University of Massachusetts Press, 1999), plus *Aard-vark to Axolotl* (Etruscan Press, 2018), a collection of tiny stories and essays inspired by the illustrations in a vintage Webster's dictionary. She is co-founder of *Paragraph,* a journal of literary short prose that published hundreds of innovative writers for 20 years and is now archived at the John Hay Library at Brown University.

Denise Duhamel's most recent book of poetry is *Scald* (Pittsburgh, 2017). A recipient of fellowships from the Guggenheim Foundation and the National Endowment for the Arts, she is a professor at Florida International University in Miami.

Jamey Dunham is the author of *The Bible of Lost Pets* (Salt Modern Poets, 2009) and co-editor of *An Introduction to the Prose Poem* (Firewheel Editions, 2009) with poet Brian Clements.

Stuart Dybek's most recent collection of verse poetry is *Streets in Their Own Ink* (FSG, 2014). *Ecstatic Cahoots* (FSG, 2014), a book of prose poems, flash fiction, and short prose appeared in 2014. Dybek is currently the distinguished writer in residence at Northwestern University.

Russell Edson accurately and jokingly referred to himself as "Big Mr. Prose Poem." Responsible for influencing just about every author in this anthology, he wrote many books over the years, including *The Reason Why the Closet-Man Is Never Sad* (Wesleyan, 1997), *The Tormented Mirror* (U. Pittsburgh Press, 2001), and *The Tunnel: Selected Poems* (Oberlin Press, 1994).

Beth Ann Fennelly, Poet Laureate of Mississippi, has won grants from the N.E.A., the United States Artists, and a Fulbright to Brazil. She has published three poetry books: *Open House, Tender Hooks,* and *Unmentionables,* and a book of nonfiction, *Great with Child,* all published with W. W. Norton, plus a novel with her husband, Tom Franklin, called *The Tilted World* (HarperCollins, 2013). Her sixth book is *Heating & Cooling: 52 Micro-Memoirs* (W. W. Norton, 2017).

Gerald Fleming's most recent book is *One,* an experiment in monosyllabic prose poems, from Hanging Loose Press. Previous books have included *The Choreographer, Night of Pure Breathing, Swimmer Climbing onto Shore,* and others.

Carolyn Forché is the author of four books of poetry. Her memoir, *What You Have Heard Is True,* was published by Penguin Press in 2019. Her fifth book of poetry, *In The Lateness of the World,* will appear the following year.

Charles Fort is the author of six books of poetry and ten chapbooks. Fort has poems in *The Best American Poetry* 2000, 2003, and 2017 and the *Best of the Prose Poem: An International Journal.* His first novel, *The Last Black Hippie in Connecticut,* will be published in 2020.

Stephen Frech has published a mixed genre chapbook, *A Palace of Strangers Is No City,* and three volumes of poetry, most recently the chapbook *The Dark Villages of Childhood.* He is also the translator of Menno Wigman's *Zwart als kaviaar/Black as Caviar.*

Jeff Friedman's seventh book of poems, *Floating Tales,* was published by Plume Editions/MadHat Press in 2017. Friedman's poems, mini stories and translations have appeared in *American Poetry Review, Poetry, New England Review, Poetry International, Plume, Agni Online, The New Republic,* and numerous other literary magazines. He is at poetjefffriedman.com.

Elisabeth Frost is the author of *All of Us* (White Pine Press), *Rumor* (Mermaid Tenement Press), *A Theory of the Vowel* (Red Glass Books), *Bindle* (Ricochet Editions, a collaboration with artist Dianne Kornberg), and *The Feminist Avant-Garde in American Poetry* (Iowa). She edits the Poets Out Loud Prizes book series from Fordham Press. ElisabethFrost.net.

Richard Garcia's *The Other Odyssey,* from Dream Horse Press, and *The Chair,* from BOA, were both published in 2015. *Porridge,* a book of prose poems, was published by Press 53 in 2016.

Amy Gerstler has published thirteen books of poems. *Scattered at Sea,* a book of her poems published by Penguin in 2015, was longlisted for the National Book Award, shortlisted for the Kingsley Tufts Award, and was a finalist for the PEN USA Literary Award. She was awarded a Guggenheim Fellowship in 2018, and in 2010 she was guest editor of *Best American Poetry.*

Ray Gonzalez received a 2017 Witter Bynner Fellowship from the Library of Congress. He is the author of fifteen books of poetry, including the recent *Beautiful Wall* (BOA Editions, 2016 Minnesota Book Award).

Daniel Grandbois lives on a mountaintop in Colorado and has written several books, including *A Revised Poetry of Western Philosophy* (Pitt Poetry Series, 2016). His work has appeared in *Fiction, Boulevard, Mississippi Review, Conjunctions* and *Electric Lit,* among others, and often includes collaborations with visual artists across the Americas.

Cathryn Hankla is the author of fourteen books in several genres including *Lost Places: On losing and finding home, Galaxies, Great Bear, Fortune Teller Miracle Fish,* and a collection of prose poems, *Texas School Book Depository* (LSU Press, 2000). She teaches in the Jackson Center for Creative Writing, serves as Poetry Editor of *The Hollins Critic,* and chairs the English & Creative Writing Department at Hollins University.

Marie Harris was New Hampshire Poet Laureate 1999–2004. She is the author of five collections of poetry and three children's books, and the editor, with Kathleen Aguero, of *An Ear to the Ground* (Univ. of Georgia Press, 1989), a multicultural poetry anthology.

Bob Heman has been writing prose poems regularly since 1973. His most recent collection is *The House of Grand Farewells* (Luna Bisonte Prods, 2019). Two earlier collections of his prose poems, *How It All Began* and *Demographics, or, The Hats They Are Allowed to Wear* are available as free downloads from Quale Press.

Holly Iglesias' work includes three collections of poetry—*Sleeping Things* (Press 53, 2018), *Angles of Approach* (White Pine Press, 2010), and *Souvenirs of a Shrunken World* (Kore Press, 2012)—and a critical study, *Boxing Inside the Box: Women's Prose Poetry* (Quale Press, 2004). She has translated the work of Cuban poets Caridad Atencio and Nicolás Padrón and received fellowships from the National Endowment for the Arts, the North Carolina Arts Council, the Edward Albee Foundation, and the Massachusetts Cultural Council.

Louis Jenkins has been writing prose poems since the 1970s. His selected prose poems can be found in *Before You Know It: Prose Poems 1970–2005* (Will o' the Wisp Books, 2009).

Brian Johnson is the author of *Torch Lake and Other Poems* (Webdelsol Press, 2008), a finalist for the Norma Farber first book prize, and *Site Visits,* a collaboration with the German painter Burghard Müller-Dannhausen. He directs the Composition Program at Southern Connecticut State University.

Peter Johnson's new book of prose poems, *Old Man Howling at the Moon,* was published by MadHat Press in 2018. His second book of prose poems, *Miracles & Mortifications* (White Pine Press, 2001), received the James Laughlin Award, and his prose poetry has also been awarded fellowships from the NEA and Rhode Island Council on the Arts. He can be found at peterjohnsonauthor.com.

Alice Jones's books include *The Knot* and *Isthmus* from Alice James Books, *Extreme Directions* (Omnidawn, 2002), and *Gorgeous Mourning* (2004) and *Plunge* (2012) from Apogee Press. The recipient of awards from the Poetry Society of America, *Narrative Magazine,* and fellowships from Bread Loaf and the NEA, she works as a psychoanalyst in Berkeley.

George Kalamaras, former Poet Laureate of Indiana (2014–2016), is the author of eighteen books of poetry and prose poetry, eleven of which are full-length, including *Kingdom of Throat-Stuck Luck* (2011), winner of the Elixir Press Prize, and *The Theory and Function of Mangoes* (2000), winner of the Four Way Books Intro Series. He is Professor of English at Purdue University–Fort Wayne, where he has taught since 1990.

Christopher Kennedy is the author of *Clues from the Animal Kingdom,* (BOA Editions, Ltd., 2018), and four other collections of poetry. He is the recipient of the Isabella Gardner Award for Poetry and a National Endowment for the Arts Fellowship for Poetry, and he is a professor of English at Syracuse University where he directs the MFA Program in Creative Writing.

Christine Boyka Kluge is the author of *Teaching Bones to Fly* (2003) and *Stirring the Mirror* (2007), both from Bitter Oleander Press. Her prose poems appear in *No Boundaries: Prose Poems by 24 American Poets,* edited by Ray Gonzalez, from Tupelo Press.

Mary A. Koncel's latest book of prose poems, *The Last Blonde* (2017), was recently published by Hedgerow Books/Levellers Press. Her other collections are *Closer to Day* (Quale Press, 1999) and *You Can Tell the Horse Anything* (Tupelo Press, 2003), which was a finalist for the Poetry Society of America's Norma Farber First Book Award.

Gerry LaFemina is the author of numerous collections of poems and prose poems, including *The Story of Ash* (Anhinga Press, 2018) and *Notes for the Novice Ventriloquist* (prose poems) (Mayapple Press, 2013). He is an Associate Professor at Frostburg State University and serves as a mentor in the Carlow University Low Residence MFA program.

David Lehman is the editor of *Great American Prose Poems* and *The Oxford Book of American Poetry.* Recent books include *Poems in the Manner of* (2017) and *Sinatra's Century: One Hundred Notes on the Man and His World* (2015). *One Hundred Autobiographies: A Memoir* appeared in 2019.

Lesle Lewis is the author of five books of prose poems; the most recent, *Rainy Days on the Farm* (Fence Books, 2019). She lives in the New Hampshire woods.

P. H. Liotta received the Robert H. Winner Memorial Award and an NEA for his poetry. His *Graveyard of Fallen Monuments* (Quale Press, 2007), his last book of prose poems, was published shortly before he was tragically killed in a car accident.

Gian Lombardo has published six collections of prose poetry, the latest of which are *Machines We Have Built* (Quale Press, 2014) and *Who Lets Go First* (Swamp Press, 2010). His translation of the first half of Aloysius Bertrand's *Gaspard de la nuit* was published in 2000, and a translation of Eugène Savitzkaya's *Rules of Solitude* in 2004, as well as translations of Archestratos's

Gastrology (2009), and Michel Delville's *Third Body* (2009) and *Anything & Everything* (2016). He teaches book and magazine publishing at Emerson College, and also directs Quale Press.

Robert Hill Long was raised and educated in the South, where his ancestors have lived since the 1650s, and now cultivates Candide's garden in a little cowtown on the Lost Coast of Northern California. He most recently published *Walking Wounded,* a book about war and surviving (WordTech Editions, out of print) and *The Kilim Dreaming* (Bear Star Press, 2010), a book of four elegiac sonnet sequences.

Morton Marcus published over eleven volumes of poetry. His prose poems were collected in *Moments Without Names: New & Selected Prose Poems* (Hanging Loose Press, 2002) and his last book of poems was *The Dark Figure in the Doorway: Last Poems* (White Pine Press, 2010).

Peter Markus is the author of the novel *Bob, or Man on Boat* (2008) as well as the collections of short fiction *The Fish and the Not Fish* (2014), *We Make Mud* (2010), *The Singing Fish* (2006), and *Good, Brother* (2001) He lives in Michigan and is the Senior Writer with the InsideOut Literary Arts Project in Detroit.

Michael Martone's new books are *Brooding: Arias, Choruses, Lullabies, Follies, Dirges, and a Duet* (University of Georgia Press, 2018) and *The Moon Over Wapakoneta: Fictions and Science Fictions from Indiana and Beyond* (Fiction Collective 2, 2018). He lives in Tuscaloosa and teaches at the university there.

Kathleen McGookey has published three chapbooks and four books of prose poems, most recently *Instructions for My Imposter* (2019). Her work has appeared in journals including *Crazyhorse, Epoch, Field, Ploughshares, Prairie Schooner* and *Quarterly West,* and she has received grants from the French Ministry of Foreign Affairs and the Sustainable Arts Foundation.

Campbell McGrath is the author of ten books of poetry, including *Spring Comes to Chicago, Florida Poems, Seven Notebooks,* and most recently *XX: Poems for the Twentieth Century* (Ecco Press), a Finalist for the 2017 Pulitzer Prize. His poetry has received many literary prizes, including the Kingsley Tufts Award, a Guggenheim Fellowship, and a MacArthur Fellowship. Born in Chicago, he lives with his family in Miami Beach and teaches at Florida International University, where he is the Philip and Patricia Frost Professor of Creative Writing.

Jay Meek's book of prose poems, *Windows,* was published by Carnegie Mellon University Press. For his poetry he received grants from the NEA, Guggenheim Foundatiion, and the Bush Foundation.

Shivani Mehta's work has appeared in numerous journals and her full-length book of poetry, *Useful Information for the Soon-to-be Beheaded* (2013), is out from Press 53. Born in Mumbai, raised in Singapore, Shivani lives near Los Angeles with her family.

Christopher Merrill has published six collections of poetry, including *Watch Fire,* for which he received the Lavan Younger Poets Award from the Academy of American Poets, and six books of nonfiction, most recently *Self-Portrait with Dogwood.* He directs the International Writing Program at the University of Iowa.

Robert Miltner is the author of the prose poetry collections *Hotel Utopia* (2011) selected by Tim Seibles for the New Rivers Press for the Many Voices Project poetry award, and *Orpheus & Echo,* forthcoming in 2019 from Etruscan Press in the three-book collective, *Triptych.* He is on the faculty of the NEOMFA and is emeritus professor at Kent State University Stark.

Naomi Shihab Nye's most recent books are *Voices in the Air: Poems for Listeners* (Greenwillow Books, 2018), *The Turtle of Oman, Transfer,* and *Famous.*

John Olson is the author of a number of books of prose poetry, including *Dada Budapest, Larynx Galaxy,* and *Backscatter: New and Selected Poems.* He is also the author of four novels, including *In Advance of the Broken Justy, The Seeing Machine, The Nothing That Is,* and *Souls of Wind.*

Pushcart Prize recipient, translator, and a founding editor of Four Way Books, **Dzvinia Orlowsky** is the author of six poetry collections published by Carnegie Mellon University Press including her most recent, *Bad Harvest,* named a 2019 Massachusetts Book Awards "Must Read" in Poetry.

Robert Perchan has prose poems in recent issues of *Crack the Spine, Spillway, Atticus Review* and other places. You can read more of his stuff at robertperchan.com.

Jane Lunin Perel is Professor Emerita of English and Women's Studies at Providence College, '15 Hon. She has written four books of free verse poetry; *Red Radio Heart* (2012) is her first book of prose poetry, and she is not done yet.

Mary Ruefle's latest book is *My Private Property* (Wave Books, 2016). She lives in Vermont.

Maureen Seaton is the author of numerous solo and collaborative poetry collections, most recently *Fisher* (Black Lawrence Press, 2018). A professor of creative writing (University of Miami, Florida), her awards include the Lambda Literary, NEA, and Pushcart.

David Shumate is the author of three books of prose poems: *High Water Mark* (2004), *The Floating Bridge* (2008), and *Kimonos in the Closet* (2013), all published by the University of Pittsburgh Press.

Charles Simic has published numerous books of his own poetry, eight books of essays, a memoir, and many books of translations of French, Serbian, Croatian, Macedonian and Slovenian poetry for which he has received literary awards, including the Pulitzer Prize, the Griffin Prize, the MacArthur Fellowship, and the Wallace Stevens Award from the Academy of American Poets. Simic was the Poet Laureate of the United States 2007–2008. *Scribbled in the Dark,* his new volume of poetry, and *The Life of Images,* a book of his selected prose are his most recent publications. His book of prose poems, *The World Doesn't End,* received the Pulitzer Prize in 1990.

Thomas R. Smith lives in western Wisconsin and teaches at the Loft Literary Center in Minneapolis. His new and selected prose poems, *Windy Day at Kabekona* (2018), is published by White Pine Press. He is also editor of *Airmail: The Letters of Robert Bly and Tomas Tranströmer* (Graywolf). He posts poems and essays at thomasrsmithpoet.com.

Liz Waldner's most recent books are *Little House, Big House (Now How I Am An American)* (Noemi Press) and *Her Faithfulness* (University of Miami Press), both published in 2016. In 2017, she received the inaugural Dorothea Tanning Award from the Foundation for Contemporary Arts.

Rosmarie Waldrop's recent books are *Gap Gardening: Selected Poems* (New Directions, 2016) and *Driven to Abstraction* (New Directions, 2010). Her novel *The Hanky of Pippin's Daughter* is newly available from Dorothy a Publishing Project; her collected essays, *Dissonance (if you are interested),* from U. of Alabama Press. She has translated 14 volumes of Edmond Jabès's work (her memoir, *Lavish Absence: Recalling and Rereading Edmond Jabès,* is out from Wesleyan University Press) as well as volumes by Emmanuel Hocquard, Jacques Roubaud, and, from the German, Friederike Mayröcker,

Elke Erb, Peter Waterhouse, Gerhard Rühm. With Keith Waldrop, she edited Burning Deck Press.

Charles Harper Webb's latest collection of poems, *Sidebend World,* was published by the University of Pittsburgh Press in 2018. *A Million MFAs Are Not Enough,* a gathering of Webb's essays on contemporary American poetry, was published in 2016 by Red Hen Press.

Tom Whalen's recent books include the novel *The President in Her Towers* (Ellipsis Press, 2013) and a translation of Robert Walser's *Girlfriends, Ghosts, and Other Stories* (*New York Review of Books* Classics, 2016). He lives in Stuttgart, Germany, and is completing a second collection of Robert Walser's prose pieces.

A writer in multiple modes, **Peter Wortsman** is the author, most recently, of a bilingual German-English book of his stories originally written in German, *Stimme und Atem / Out of Breath, Out of Mind* (Palm Art Press, Berlin, 2019); a second edition of his first book of short enigmatic prose, *A Modern Way to Die,* with a prefatory note by the late Hubert Selby, Jr. (Pelekinesis, 2019); a book of nonfiction, *The Caring Heirs of Doctor Samuel Bard* (Columbia University Press, 2019); and the English translations of *Intimate Ties,* by Robert Musil (Archipelago Books, 2019) and *Hinkemann,* a tragedy by German Expressionist playwright Ernst Toller (Berlinica Books, 2019). The recipient of an Independent Publishers Book Award (IPPY) in 2014 for his travel memoir *Ghost Dance in Berlin* (2013), he was a Holtzbrinck Fellow at the American Academy in Berlin in 2010.

Gary Young is a poet and artist whose most recent books are *That's What I Thought* (2018), winner of the Lexi Rudnitsky Editor's Choice Award from Persea Books, and *Precious Mirror,* translations from the Japanese published by White Pine Press. His many honors include the Shelley Memorial Award and the William Carlos Williams Award, and he received grants from the National Endowment for the Humanities, two fellowship grants from the National Endowment for the Arts, the California Arts Council, and the Vogelstein Foundation, among others.

Acknowledgments

A special thanks to Marc Vincenz: talented poet, fiction writer, translator and editor, who saw the value of publishing this anthology, and whose vision and work ethic continues to inspire me.

—*PJ*

Kim Addonizio: "Watch," from *Jimmy & Rita,* BOA Editions, 1997; reissued by Stephen F. Austin State University Press, 2012. Copyright 1997, 2012 by Kim Addonizio. Used by permission of the author.

Robert Alexander: "Only in Retrospect," from *What the Raven Said.* Used by permission of the author. Commentary modified from "Afterword: Supple and Jarring," *Family Portrait: American Prose Poetry, 1900–1950.* Used by permission of the author.

John Allman: "Lunch," from *Algorithms,* Quale Press, 2012. Used by permission of the author.

Jack Anderson: "The Marriage of the Summer Hours." Reprinted from *Backyards of the Universe* (2017) by permission of Hanging Loose Press.

Nin Andrews: "Spontaneous Breasts," from *Spontaneous Breasts,* Pearl Editions, 1998. Poem and commentary also from *The Prose Poem: An International Journal,* Volume 8, 1999. Reprinted by permission of the author.

Sally Ashton: "Gratitude" first appeared in the publication *sparkle&blink.* Reprinted by permission of the author.

Michael Benedikt: "The Doorway of Perception," from *Night Cries,* Wesleyan University Press, 1976. Poem and commentary also from *The Prose Poem: An International Journal,* Volume 8, 1999.

Robert Bly: "Warning to the Reader," from *The Prose Poem: An International Journal,* Volume 1, 1991. Reprinted by permission of the author.

Greg Boyd: "Edouard's Nose," from *Carnival Aptitude,* Asylum Arts. 1993. Poem and commentary also from *The Prose Poem: An International Journal,* Volume 8, 1999. Reprinted by permission of the author.

John Bradley: "Mortal Colors," from *The Rockhurst Review,* Volume 10, Spring 1997. Poem and commentary also from *The Prose Poem: An International Journal,* Volume 8, 1999. Reprinted by permission of the author.

Joel Brouwer: "Aesthetics," from *Centuries,* Four Way Books, 2003 by Joel Brouwer. Reprinted with permission of Four Way Books. All rights reserved.

Mairéad Byrne: "The Russian Week" was first published in *The Denver Quarterly* 40.2 (2005). Reprinted by permission of the author

Maxine Chernoff: "Singular" is from *Here,* Counterpath Press, 2014. Reprinted by permission of the author.

Laura Chester: This poem was published in *Free Rein,* Burning Deck, 1988, and was also included in *Sparks,* The Figures Press, 2010. Reprinted by permission of the author.

Kim Chinquee: "Milk" used by permission of *Cream City Review.*

Brian Clements: "Dream Letter" originally appeared in *Essays Against Ruin,* Texas Review Press, 1997. Reprinted by permission of the author.

Peter Conners: "A Man Learns to Fly" appeared in the collection *Of Whiskey & Winter,* White Pine Press, 2007. Reprinted by permission of the author.

Jon Davis. "The Bait," reprinted by permission of the author.

Peter Davis: "Hitler's Mustache: The Short Story," from *Hitler's Mustache* by Peter Davis, Barnwood Press, 2006. Reprinted by permission of the author.

Michel Delville: "Marcel Duchamp," from *Anything & Everything: Prose Poems and Microessays,* Quale Press, 2016. Translated from the French by Gian Lombardo. Reprinted by permission of the author.

Chard deNiord: "The Music," from *The Prose Poem: An International Journal.* Reprinted by permission of the author.

Karen Donovan: "Spirits," from *Aard-vark to Axolotl: Pictures from My Grandfather's Dictionary,* reprinted with the permission of Etruscan Press. Illustration used by permission. From *Webster's New International Dictionary of the English Language,* 1925, Merriam-Webster, Inc.

Denise Duhamel: "Scalding Cauldron," from *Scald,* University of Pittsburgh Press. 2017. Reprinted by permission of the author.

Jamey Dunham: "Trickster at the Free Clinic," from *The Bible of Lost Pets,* Salt Modern Poets, 2009. Reprinted by permission of the author.

Stuart Dybek: "Inland Sea," reprinted from *Ecstatic Cahoots,* FSG, 2014. Reprinted by permission of the author.

Russell Edson: "The Tunnel," from *The Tunnel: Selected Poems of Russell Edson,* Oberlin College Press, 1994. Poem and commentary also from *The Prose Poem: An International Journal,* Volume 7, 1998.

Beth Ann Fennelly: "What I Think About When Someone Uses 'Pussy' as a Synonym for 'Weak'," from *Heating & Cooling: 52 Micro-Memoirs.* Used by permission of W. W. Norton & Co.

Gerald Fleming: "Crucifixion, Kinetic," reprinted from *The Choreographer,* Sixteen Rivers Press, San Francisco, 2013. Reprinted by permission of the author.

Carolyn Forché: "The Colonel," reprinted by permission of HarperCollins and the author.

Charles Fort: "Requiem for the Twenty-First Century" was previously published in *Callaloo, Frankenstein Was a Negro,* Backwaters Press, *Mrs. Belladonna's Supper Club Waltz, New and Selected Prose Poems,* Backwaters Press, and *We Did Not Fear the Father, New and Selected Poems,* Red Hen Press, 2012. A portion of the prose poem was first published in *Callaloo* as "Darvil Meets James Brown in Harlem and New Orleans."

Stephen Frech: Section 10 from *A Palace of Strangers Is No City,* Červená Barva Press, 2011. Used by permission of the author.

Jeff Friedman: "Judges," from *Floating Tales,* Plume Editions/MadHat Press, 2017, and from *Pretenders,* reprinted with permission of Carnegie Mellon University Press, 2014. Reprinted by permission of the author.

Elisabeth Frost: "New Story," from *Electronic Poetry Review* 8 (2008). Reprinted by permission of the author.

Richard Garcia: "Chickenhead," from *The Best of the Prose Poem: An International Journal.* Reprinted by permission of the author.

Amy Gerstler: "Bitter Angel," from the book of the same title, first published by North Point Press in 1990; reprinted by Carnegie Mellon University in 1997. Poem and commentary also from *The Prose Poem: An International Journal,* Volume 8, 1999. Reprinted by permission of the author.

Ray Gonzalez: "Seams," published here for the first time.

Daniel Grandbois: "On First Looking Into Campbell's Chunky," published here for the first time.

Cathryn Hankla: "What Falls," published here for the first time.

Marie Harris: This poem appeared in the prose poem anthology *The Party Train,* New Rivers Press, 1996. Reprinted by permission of the author.

Bob Heman: "Perfect" was first published in the 2008 *Brownstone Poets Anthology* and was later reprinted in the anthology *The Venetian Hour,* Ra Rays Press, 2014. Reprinted by permission of the author.

Holly Iglesias: "Perishables," from *Angles of Approach*, White Pine Press, Marie Alexander Series, 2010. First published in *Margie: The American Journal of Poetry*, Vol. 4, 2005. Reprinted by permission of the author.

Louis Jenkins: "Basketball," from *An Almost Human Gesture,* The Eighties Press and Ally Press, 1987. Poem and commentary also from *The Prose Poem: An International Journal,* Volume 8, 1999. Reprinted by permission of the author.

Brian Johnson: "Scenes of Disaster," published here for the first time.

Peter Johnson: "The Millennium," from *Pretty Happy!,* White Pine Press, 1997. Reprinted by permission of the author.

Alice Jones: "Reply." Reprinted from *Gorgeous Mourning*, 2004, by permission of Apogee Press

George Kalamaras: "A Father Kisses His Daughter Goodbye," from *Calibanonline,* Issue 21, October 2015. Reprinted by permission of the author.

Christopher Kennedy: "Some Other Species of Love," from *Clues from the Animal Kingdom,* BOA Editions, Ltd., 2018. Reprinted by permission of the author.

Christine Boyka Kluge: "Where Babies Come From," from *Stirring the Mirror,* Bitter Oleander Press, 2007. It first appeared in *Quarterly West,* Spring/ Summer 2000. Reprinted by permission of the author.

Mary Koncel: "After the Weather," from *The Prose Poem: An International Journal,* Volume 2, 1993. Poem and commentary also from *The Prose Poem: An International Journal,* Volume 8, 1999. Reprinted by permission of the author.

Gerry Lafemina: "Thinking of You," published here for the first time.

David Lehman: "Mother Died Today," from *New and Selected Poems,* Scribner, 2013. Reprinted by permission of the author.

Lesle Lewis: "When 'Towns, Cities, and Villages Disappeared from the Earth'," published here for the first time.

P. H. Liotta: "The Blue Whale," from *Graveyard of the Fallen Monuments,* Quale Press, 2007. Poem and commentary also from *The Prose Poem: An International Journal,* Volume 8, 1999.

Gian Lombardo: Poem and commentary from *The Prose Poem: An International Journal,* Volume 7, 1999. Reprinted by permission of the author.

Robert Hill Long: An earlier version of "*Malpensa, Outbound*" appeared in *Noctua* (Southern Connecticut University, 2014). I dedicate it here to the memory of Will Gardner, student and friend, who solicited it for that publication.

Morton Marcus: "The Canary Islands," from *When People Could Fly,* Hanging Loose Press, 1997. Poem and commentary also from *The Prose Poem: An International Journal,* Volume 8, 1999.

Peter Markus: "Light" first appeared in *The Prose Poem: An International Journal,* and is used by permission of the author.

Michael Martone: "The Mayor of the Sister City Talks to the Chamber of Commerce in Klamath Falls, Oregon" won the inaugural World's Greatest Short Short Story Prize and was published in *Sun Dog* 7:2 (1986). Used by permission of the author.

Kathleen McGookey: "Ordinary Objects, Extraordinary Emotions," from *Heart in a Jar,* White Pine Press, 2017. Used with permission of the publisher.

Campbell McGrath: "Rifle, Colorado," used by permission of the author.

Jay Meek: "Travel Notes," from *Windows,* Carnegie-Mellon University Press, 1994. Poem and commentary also from *The Prose Poem: An International Journal,* Volume 7, 1999.

Shivani Mehta: "This Is How I learned About Regret," published here for the first time.

Christopher Merrill: "Notes for a Dance," published here for the first time.

Robert Miltner: "Wolf Dancing is Back," used by permission of the author.

Naomi Shihab Nye: "His Life," from *Mint,* State Street Press, 1991. Poem and commentary also from *The Prose Poem: An International Journal,* Volume 7, 1999. Reprinted by permission of the author.

John Olson: "Kierkegaard at Home Depot" is from *Dada Budapest,* Black Widow Press, 2017 and also in the journal *House Organ,* in which it first appeared. Reprinted by permission of the author.

Dzvinia Orlowsky: "Vegreville Egg" was published in *Plume* 5, 2017. Used by permission of the author.

Robert Perchan: "Neandertal Hotline" and commentary, from *The Prose Poem: An International Journal,* Volume 8, 1999. Reprinted by permission of the author.

Jane Lunin Perel: "Red Radio Heart," from *Red Radio Heart,* White Pine Press, 2012. Used by permission of White Pine Press.

Mary Ruefle: "Please Read," from *My Private Property,* Wave Books, 2016. Reprinted by permission of the author.

Maureen Seaton: "Fisher" was previously published in *Fisher*, Black Lawrence Press, 2018. Reprinted here with permission of the press and the author.

David Shumate: "End of the Year," from *Lake Effect.* Reprinted by permission of the author.

Charles Simic: "I was stolen by the gypsies," from *The World Doesn't End,* Harcourt Brace & Company, 1989. Reprinted by permission of the author.

Thomas R. Smith: "Brushpile Sparrows," from *Windy Day at Kabekona: New and Selected Prose Poems,* White Pine Press, 2018. Reprinted by permission of the author.

Liz Waldner: "Now How I Am An American" is from the collection *Little House, Big House (Now How I Am An American),* Noemi Press, 2016, and used by their kind permission.

Rosmarie Waldrop: From *Lawn of the Excluded Middle,* Tender Buttons Press, 1993. Poem and commentary also from *The Prose Poem: An International Journal,* Volume 7, 1998. Reprinted by permission of the author.

Charles Harper Webb: "Handsome Can Sit Up by Himself" is published here for the first time.

Tom Whalen: "The Doll Writes to Her Mother," from *Dolls,* Caketrain, 2007. Reprinted by permission of the author.

Peter Wortsman: "The Back of Words" originally appeared as a postscript to his translation *Kondundrum, Selected Prose of Franz Kafka,* Archipelago Books, 2016. Reprinted by permission of the author.

Gary Young: "Finding the Poem: Some Notes on Form," from *Silverfish Review* 27/28, 1996. Poem and commentary also from *The Prose Poem: An International Journal,* Volume 8, 1999. Reprinted by permission of the author. Poem from *Even So: New and Selected Poems,* White Pine Press, 2012.

I wish to thank all the poets and publishers who made this anthology possible. And a special thanks to MadHat Press and Marc Vincenz—poet, fiction writer, translator, editor and publisher—who had the vision and patience to take on this project.

—PJ

CPSIA information can be obtained
at www.ICGtesting.com
Printed in the USA
LVHW031122200120
644155LV00007B/1095

9 781941 196922